ONE NEW MAN

ONE NEW MAN

A COMMENTARY ON GALATIANS AND EPHESIANS

DOUGLAS WILSON

CA NON PRESS

MOSCOW, IDAHO

Douglas Wilson, *One New Man: A Commentary on Galatians and Ephesians*
Copyright © 2022 by Douglas Wilson

Published by Canon Press
P. O. Box 8729, Moscow, Idaho 83843
800-488-2034 | www.canonpress.com

Cover design by James Engerbretson
Interior design by Valerie Anne Bost
Printed in the United States of America

All Scripture quotations are from the King James Version.

Library of Congress Cataloging-in-Publication Data:
Wilson, Douglas, 1953- author.
One new man : a commentary on Galatians and Ephesians / Douglas Wilson.
Moscow, Idaho : Canon Press, 2022. | Includes bibliographical references.
LCCN 2022002188 | ISBN 9781954887169 (paperback)
LCSH: Bible. Galatians—Commentaries. | Bible. Ephesians—Commentaries.
Classification: LCC BS2685.53 .W5398 2022 | DDC 227/.407—dc23/eng
    /20220528
LC record available at https://lccn.loc.gov/2022002188

22 23 24 25 26 27 28 29   10 9 8 7 6 5 4 3 2 1

CONTENTS

For my mother, Bessie Wilson,
who loved the book of Ephesians.

INTRODUCTION

I f the book of Ephesians is like a treasury of Pauline doctrine, containing shelf after shelf of priceless jewels and
gems, the book of Galatians is like a firefight with the secu-
rity team in the hallway outside. Certain false brethren had
crept in in order to attempt the heist of the ages, but they
were arrested by the great apostle. Not only so, but they
were then tried and convicted by the Jerusalem Council
shortly thereafter.

Galatians is made up of both heat and light, while Ephesians is simply light. This is not a criticism of either, obviously, as both are the Word of God, perfect for their respective situations. The doctrine contained in the two books

comes from the same mind, the same heart, the same man. It is obviously consistent. But in the former you have a husband, fighting to protect his wife from assailants, and in the latter you have a husband and wife sharing a quiet dinner together, talking about what is most important to them. If someone is important to you, and you love her, you will fight for her. And if someone is important to you, and you love her, you will also talk with her. There is no inconsistency.

If there had been no fight in Galatians, then all the words of Ephesians would have been meaningless. If there had been no treasures in Ephesians, there would have been nothing to fight for.

These books are presented to you together in the hope that you will be blessed and edified, learning when to fight and when to reflect.

DOUGLAS WILSON
Christ Church
July 2023

GALATIANS

GALATIANS 1

ENTERING THE REGENERATION

It is always fitting for Christians to take any opportunity to study the book of Galatians, that great charter of Christian freedom. We need to stand fast in the liberty Christ brought to us, and we must refuse every form of sinful bondage.

> Paul, an apostle, (not of men, neither by man, but by Jesus Christ, and God the Father, who raised him from the dead;) And all the brethren which are with me, unto the churches of Galatia: Grace be to you and peace from God the Father, and from our Lord Jesus Christ, Who gave himself for our sins, that he might deliver us from this present evil world, according to the will of God and our Father: To whom be glory for ever and ever. Amen. (Gal. 1:1–5)

DATE AND LOCATION

The letter to the Galatians was written to a collection of churches in the Roman province of Galatia—churches such as Lystra, Iconium, and Derbe. Paul had gone through this area on his first missionary journey, but no sooner had he gotten back to Antioch than he discovered that false teachers were following in his wake and disrupting the churches there. Not only this, but Peter had capitulated to the same error at Antioch, causing a crisis there. All this occurred just before the Jerusalem Council (Acts 15), placing the writing of Galatians in the mid to late 40s. This is significant because it makes this classic Pauline statement of the gospel one of the *earliest* books of the New Testament. The view that Galatians was written to the believers of *ethnic* Galatia to the north cannot really be sustained.

THE DOCTRINAL RELEVANCE OF GEOGRAPHY

Some say it is "white hot." Others, "explosive and fiery," or "spiritual dynamite." I prefer to call it "blistering," but, whatever the description, the point remains the same—Paul's letter to the Galatians uses *strong* language (Gal. 1:6; 3:1; 5:12; 6:12).

So why, in the midst of this hot epistle, does Paul suddenly insert a short post-conversion autobiography and travelogue? Given the tone of the book, the obvious answer is that Paul's history has a crucial significance to the doctrinal dispute in question. Thus, from Galatians 1:11–2:14, we find a personal history of Paul which directly bears on the doctrinal apostasy that was occurring in Galatia at the time.

The issue in the Galatian churches was that certain teachers were presenting a different "gospel" (Gal. 1:6–7), which in Paul's eyes was not a gospel at all. This "gospel" entailed an attempt to be "justified by law" (Gal. 5:4). More specifically, it taught that circumcision was necessary for salvation. The Galatians were apparently unaware that this would result in alienation from Christ and bondage to the Jewish law (Gal. 5:3).

Given this situation, it is easy to see that Paul's purpose is not to simply outline his travels. It is to defend himself against the accusation that he is not a true apostle directly sent by Christ (Gal. 1:1).

My understanding of Paul's travels as described here could be labeled "South Galatian."[1] This is the view that the Galatian churches were located in the Roman province of Galatia, and not in the ethnic region of Galatia to the north. My main reason for adopting this approach is that in my view it requires the least amount of interpretation in the texts involved—in a South Galatian framework, the parallel passages in Galatians and Acts fit together in what I regard as quite a natural fashion.

With that in mind, I will try to briefly outline my understanding of Paul's actual movements and their significance. A common assumption holds that Saul was his non-Christian name and Paul his Christian name, but I believe this is mistaken. I take Saul as his Hebrew name, and Paul as the name he used when out among the Gentiles. He doesn't call himself Paul until a number of *years* after his conversion,

---

1. Donald Guthrie, *New Testament Introduction*, 3rd ed. (Downer's Grove, IL: InterVarsity Press, 1970), 450–457.

when he was presenting the gospel on his first missionary journey to Sergius Paulus (Acts 13:9). I am going to do the same kind of thing here, calling him Saul for a while before sliding into Paul.

So Saul of Tarsus was radically converted outside the city of Damascus. He was going there to imprison the Christians when God "was pleased to reveal his Son in" him (Gal. 1:15,16; cf. Acts 9:1–9). Saul immediately began proclaiming Jesus as the Christ in the Damascene synagogue (Acts 9:19–22). Although he was in Damascus for only a few days (Acts 9:19), Saul learned and grew enough in that time to baffle the Jews (Acts 9:22).

He then left for Arabia (Gal. 1:17) and, after an indefinite period of time there, returned to Damascus (Gal. 1:17). He was by now enough of a threat that the Jews in Damascus conspired to kill him (Acts 9:23). He learned of this, escaped, and made his way to Jerusalem. Saul's reception was less than cordial (Acts 9:26), but Barnabas spoke up for him (Acts 9:27). His total time in Damascus/Arabia/Damascus was about three years.

Saul's stay in Jerusalem was short—about fifteen days—but eventful. During this time, he met Peter (Gal. 1:18), and he debated with Grecian Jews (Acts 9:29) who then attempted to kill him. When the Christian brothers learned of this plot, they sent Saul back to his hometown of Tarsus (Acts 3:30; Gal. 1:21). Saul did not want to leave, yet he yielded in obedience to a vision of the Lord Jesus he had seen while praying at the temple (Acts 22:17). The Lord told him that people in Jerusalem would not listen to him, but He had another job for him—a mission to the Gentiles.

Sometime later, Barnabas was at Syrian Antioch with an oversized Gentile church on his hands. He went to Tarsus to ask Saul to help with the work (Acts 11:22–26), and Saul agreed to go.

Barnabas and Saul had spent a year in Antioch teaching the people there when they received a revelation from the Lord via the prophet Agabus that the entire Roman world would be subjected to a severe famine. With true Christian compassion, the church at Antioch decided to send a gift to the saints in Jerusalem via Barnabas and Saul (Acts 11:27–30). This was Saul's second visit to Jerusalem since his encounter with the risen Lord.

We learn that this second visit to Jerusalem was fourteen years after the first one (Gal. 2:1). Saul had spent a year at Antioch, which leaves him for thirteen years in Tarsus. It is inconceivable that a man of Saul's character would be silent about his encounter with the risen Lord during this time, so we can assume that he was preaching the gospel there.

Saul mentions the revelation that came through Agabus as his reason for being in Jerusalem at all (Gal. 2:2). While there, Saul conferred with the Jerusalem apostles concerning the nature of the gospel (Gal. 2:2). But he did this privately lest a public meeting (in which the Judaizers could have a more powerful presence) ruin the work which he had already accomplished among the Gentiles.

He rejoiced in the solidarity of the apostles. They all agreed that Titus did not require circumcision (Gal. 2:3–5). They all recognized that God was behind both Jewish and Gentile evangelism, and they extended the right hand of fellowship to each other (Gal. 2:8–9). Although Saul rejoiced in this unity, he did not make it the foundation of his mission, as we shall later see.

The only thing the Jerusalem apostles asked was that the Antioch delegation continue to remember the poor. This Saul was eager to do—it was the reason he came to Jerusalem in the first place. This was the famine relief visit, after all.

Afterward, Peter paid a visit to Antioch, which is where he had his famous run-in with Saul (Gal. 2:11–13). Saul rebuked Peter publicly for his inconsistency in not standing up to the Judaizers (Gal. 2:11, 14). Peter clearly accepted this rebuke because at the Jerusalem Council, which met shortly after this episode to discuss this issue, he very ably represents the Pauline position (Acts 15:7–11).

This is a fairly simple restatement of the South Galatian theory. The point to note in this framework is that Saul's movements as described in Acts and Galatians fit together in a *natural* way. Thus, any burden of proof should rest with the North Galatian theory, which is that Galatia refers to ethnic Galatia, which lies to the north of the Roman province of Galatia. The biggest problem with this approach is that it has to assume that Paul planted churches there during his long stint in Tarsus, or at some other time, without any New Testament reference to his travels there.

But either way, we still need to determine the reason Paul recounted his history and expected it to affect the Galatian controversy. There are two key concepts that Paul is desiring to define here. One is the nature of the gospel, and the other is the nature of apostleship.

It is often claimed that Paul wanted to assert his independence from the other apostles, as though this were important in itself.[2] I believe this is inaccurate. Paul is asserting the independence of the gospel from man—*any* man. And he is asserting the solidarity of the apostles in testifying to that same gospel.

Paul tells us plainly, "But I certify you, brethren, that the gospel which was preached of me is not after man. For I neither received it of man, neither was I taught it, but by the revelation of Jesus Christ" (Galatians 1:11–12). The first point Paul makes here is that the gospel did not originate with any human being, *including Paul.* It is of supernatural origin.

He then defends his own apostleship by denying that he was a mere convert as a result of human preaching: *I did not receive it . . . nor was I taught it . . .*

Paul then combines these two lines of thought when he says that he received it "by revelation of Jesus Christ." In saying he received it by revelation, he is continuing his brief defense of his own apostleship: he did not receive it from man but from God. In saying "of Jesus Christ," he is returning to his original point concerning the ultimate source of the gospel: the gospel is *not* man-made but rather, "according to the will of our God and our Father" (Gal. 1:4).

Paul makes an even stronger statement concerning the independence of the Gospel, though our familiarity with the words often numbs us to their forcefulness: "But though we, or an angel from heaven, preach any other gospel unto you than that which we have preached unto you, let him

2. For a mild example, see Herman Ridderbos, *The Epistles of Paul to the Churches of Galatia,* New International Commentary on the New Testament (Grand Rapids: Eerdmans, 1953), 81.

be accursed. As we said before, so say I now again, if any man preach any other gospel unto you than that ye have received, let him be accursed" (Gal. 1:8–9).

Paul is saying that this message *is radically independent of the messenger*. The gospel is not true because the apostles say so; they testify to something that is *inherently* true. Paul is saying that if he or any (or all) of the other apostles denied or changed the gospel, it would not change the facts. The gospel would remain God's truth.

This has important bearing on Galatians chapter 2, verse 6. Based on Paul's statement that those men "added nothing to me," some have assumed a certain coolness between Paul and the Jerusalem apostles, arguing that Paul wanted to maintain his independence from the Jerusalem apostles.[3] But this was not Paul's intention at all. Paul is not concerned for *Paul's* independence; he is concerned for the *gospel's* independence. He has stated this emphatically in chapter 1, and we need to remember it when we read chapter 2.

A mistaken way to read this verse would be "those men added nothing to my message, although they gave it a try. But I held my ground, and Peter, James, and John got nowhere." This view sets Paul over against the Jerusalem apostles, which then makes Paul's independence necessary. A better way to read the verse is "those men added nothing to my message; I added nothing to theirs. There was no need—we all had the same message straight from Jesus Christ. They saw that I had been given the task of

3. R.A. Cole, *The Epistle of Paul to the Galatians*, Tyndale New Testament Commentaries (Carol Stream, IL: Tyndale, 1965), 68.

preaching *the gospel* to the Gentiles, just as Peter had been given the task of preaching *the gospel* to the Jews." The gospel was the gospel and independent of *all* the apostles, including Paul.

Paul makes two assertions by mentioning those who were apostles before him (Gal. 1:17). One, he says that they are true apostles and, two, that they preceded him in that apostleship.

In chapter 2 of Galatians, the apostles' unity is seen in three areas. First, as a surprise to the Judaizers, the apostles agreed that Titus did not need to be circumcised (v. 3). Second, and related to the first, they all withstood the false brothers *together*: "To whom we gave place by subjection, no, not for an hour; that the truth of the gospel might continue with you" (Gal. 2:5). And third, the Jerusalem apostles extended the right hand of fellowship to Paul and Barnabas (v. 9).[4]

At a time when opposition to the gospel Paul preached was rampant in the Jerusalem church, the leaders of that church made it known that they preached exactly the same gospel. It would have been politically easy for the Jerusalem apostles to repudiate Paul, but they did not. This evidences a high degree of commitment to the same gospel that held Paul's allegiance.

Are there any evidences in the text that tension existed between Paul and the Jerusalem apostles? I really don't think so. Paul refers to his pestilent opponents as "certain

---

4. As Cole points out, "Clasped right hands were the sign of friendship and trust, and this action on the part of the church leaders in Jerusalem must have been a bitter blow to the Judaizers" (*Epistle of Paul*, 69).

men . . . from James" (Gal. 2:12). Were these men acting under authorization from James? In this situation I am certain that James could second the remark of John Dewey: "Lord, deliver me from my disciples!" In Acts 15:24, James helps formulate a formal denial that these men had any official sanction.

Very frequently in history we see disciples who do not have the discretionary greatness that their leaders have. Disciples make impetuous judgments, which then mushroom into extremes. Paul mentions this kind of person in 1 Corinthians: "For while one saith, I am of Paul; and another, I am of Apollos; are ye not carnal?" (1 Cor. 3:4). Paul knew of this tendency to exalt a leader as a person, while at the same time twisting his teaching.

With all of this in mind, some of Paul's earlier comments in Galatians chapter 2 become more clear. When Paul talks of "them which were of reputation" (v. 2) and says that "God accepteth no man's person" (v. 6), he is not saying anything that he does not apply to himself in equal measure as well. Paul is doing two things at one time. One, he is trying to counter a personality cult centering around the apostles, particularly those apostles who knew the Lord during His earthly ministry. Two, despite the personality cults, Paul wants to show that he and the other apostles had unbroken fellowship. He does this by identifying himself with them in the strongest possible terms and, at the same time, pointing out that the value in being an apostle has nothing to do with natural leadership or external appearance. It has to do with the gospel of the risen Christ and the apostles' testimony to that fact.

The gospel gives apostleship its value, not the other way around. Paul is simply trying to get peoples' eyes off the apostles and back to the message about the Lord. And with this, the other apostles would have been in complete agreement.

So Paul gives us his personal itinerary in Galatians for two major reasons. One is to show that the source of the gospel is Jesus Christ, not any human apostle. Paul shows how he and the other apostles had little contact early on *in order to illustrate the true basis of their unity.* That basis of unity is an encounter with the risen Lord who commissioned them all to preach the *same* message. Paul's second reason for including his history is to show that he and the other apostles are indeed preaching the same message. His objective is to silence the distortions of their teaching, which are circulating in the Church.

Given that purpose, Paul does an exemplary job of making these two major points. It is clear that, according to Paul, the gospel is unchanging, rooted in the revelation of Jesus Christ. To this fact all the apostles bear witness. Not only do the apostles all agree with this, Paul is willing to bring out his ticket stubs and boarding passes as subordinate witnesses to that same gospel. But if they did not prove that point, the gospel would still be God's truth. Let God be true and every man a liar.

PROLOGUE TO GALATIANS

Paul, an apostle, (not of men, neither by man, but by Jesus Christ, and God the Father, who raised him from

the dead;) And all the brethren which are with me, unto
the churches of Galatia: Grace be to you and peace from
God the Father, and from our Lord Jesus Christ, Who
gave himself for our sins, that he might deliver us from
this present evil world, according to the will of God and
our Father: To whom be glory for ever and ever. Amen.
(Gal. 1:1–5)

As we consider Paul's argument throughout this book, we
see him answering objections to his position that had been
raised by his adversaries. He answers one of them in his first
breath. His apostleship was either denied by his adversaries, or it was claimed that his apostleship was secondary
and derivative. He was called a "second-generation" apostle, and he meets this head-on in the first verse. He was an
apostle in the strongest sense of that word—not by men, not
by a man, but by Jesus Christ, and God the Father, who had
raised Jesus from the dead. Paul was an apostle of resurrection power, an apostle of the liberty new life gives. He was
therefore not going to submit to a "compromise" between
life and death.

The letter was probably written from Antioch, and it was
not just from Paul. Salutations at the ends of letters are
simply greetings, but people named at the beginning are
those who are helping to speak authoritatively. Paul is writing from the Galatians' mother church, and many brothers
were there who were with Paul on this issue. The letter is
addressed to multiple churches.

Despite the consternation Paul feels about what the Galatians are doing, he gives his customary blessing—grace and

peace from God the Father, and from our Lord Jesus Christ (v. 3). The glory resulting from the great work of salvation is glory that will be accorded to the Father forever and ever (v. 5). Amen. The controversy at Galatia is crucial but does not prevent Paul from blessing them, and he does not forget to bless God the Father in faith.

Before Paul gets into the particular aspects of the controversy, he sets the stage for a right understanding of that controversy in his comments of verse 4. Grace and peace come from the Lord Jesus, who gave Himself for our sins (v. 4). He did this so that He might deliver us from this present evil age (v. 4), and this was all done in accord with the will of God the Father (v. 4).

Now, God has made all things new. As we consider this, we need to consider the following three things in some detail. First, our salvation was accomplished by the will of the Father. It was not done on a whim, or a last-minute thought. When Jesus went to the cross, He was submitting to the will of the Father, and, in doing this, He was securing our salvation in full accordance with that will.

Secondly, "our sins" are a significant part of what is dealt with in the work of redemption, but they are by no means the entire picture. After all, Jesus gave Himself for our sins, as it says here. But it says this was done in order to accomplish something else.

That something else is the third point, which was the Father's intention to deliver us from the present evil age. Now what does this mean? *When* was this done? Answering these questions rightly helps us put the gospel of Jesus Christ in cosmic perspective. In other words, unless there is a new heavens and new earth, there will be no new hearts. Jesus referred to the regeneration of the cosmos (Matt. 19:28), and the apostle Paul spoke of individual regeneration (Titus 3:5). The regeneration has entered us because we have entered the Regeneration.

THE WRONG LINE OF WORK

After a brief introduction and greetings, Paul raises the issue that is troubling *him*, and that is the fact that someone is troubling the Galatians. Not only this, but they are not being troubled on some secondary issue. The gospel itself is at stake.

> I marvel that ye are so soon removed from him that called you into the grace of Christ unto another gospel: which is not another; but there be some that trouble you, and would pervert the gospel of Christ. But though we, or an angel from heaven, preach any other gospel unto you than that which we have preached unto you, let him be accursed. As we said before, so say I now again, If any man preach any other gospel unto you than that ye have received, let him be accursed. For do I now persuade men, or God? or do I seek to please men? for if I yet pleased men, I should not be the servant of Christ. (Gal. 1:6–10)

We are accustomed in Christian circles to speak of God's amazing grace. But something else that is amazing is how quickly Christians can drift away from this amazing grace.

Call it amazing drift. And Paul marvels at it—how *readily* the Galatians were unsettled! How quickly they were removed from the Father, the one who had called them into the grace of Christ (v. 6). And when they began to be removed from the true gospel, they went to the only alternative, which was a false gospel.

Of course, another gospel cannot really be another gospel—there cannot be more than one of them (v. 7). And this means that this new and improved gospel is actually a turning aside from the gospel; it is perversion. Moreover, such perversions are no accident. When there is perversion, there is a pervert. "Someone" was troubling the Galatians.

The benchmark against which everything else was to be measured was the gospel that had been preached to the Galatians at the first. Paul says this in two ways— "that which we have preached unto you" (v. 8) and "that ye have received" (v. 9). This primitive gospel outranks everyone, whether the emissary is apostolic or angelic. It *certainly* outranked the false brothers who were troubling the Galatians.

The false teachers were doubly damned. So adamant is Paul about this that he repeats his grave *anathema* twice, and he does this deliberately for emphasis. There is even an indication that Paul may have said this before, when he was with the Galatians. The gospel is not something that men have the authority to alter or improve, or adjust to fit with the times. Anyone who attempts this falls under the divine curse. An angel or an apostle who sets himself against the gospel will be condemned under the reign of the gospel. This is not the kind of difference that allows for dialog with alternative perspectives, or provides any basis for a search for common ground.

With this attitude, it was plain that if Paul was wanting to be a man-pleaser, he was in the wrong line of work. Who was Paul trying to persuade? Was he trying to persuade men or God? Who was he trying to please, men or God? He makes it very plain that if he wanted to be a man-pleaser, he made the wrong choice in becoming a servant of Christ (v. 10). The two do not abide together, and cannot. But let it be said at the same time that there *are* carnal ways to displease men, and let us even emphasize it. But the point that has to be made from *this* text is that anyone who wishes to be a faithful servant of Christ *will* incur the enmity of men. Moreover, when that enmity is incurred, the adversary will *not* say that it is because of faithfulness to Christ. The claim against Paul was that he got his apostleship from men, which he hotly denied (Gal. 1:12). He was also accused of setting aside the law of Moses, along with lots of other things he shouldn't have done. The verbal weapons employed against God's servants *are not the reason for the war.* Too many Christians forget that the devil lies.

So what do we discover here? What words of encouragement can we take away from this? We have been privileged to have drawn the fire of the enemy. We have risen to the dignity of needing to be opposed. We have the great honor of needing to be lied about. From all this, we must take solace and encouragement. But, like the Hebrews, we have not yet resisted to the shedding of blood. We are discovering that the parade after boot camp and engagement with the enemy are two different things. We are discovering that it is one thing to come home on leave and have all the girls admire your uniform, and quite another to enter into the chaos and confusion of battle.

GOSPEL AS APOCALYPSE

We now come to one of the great claims made in this epistle. The gospel is divine, not man-made, and this truth involves much more than might be assumed at first glance.

> But I certify you, brethren, that the gospel which was preached of me is not after man. For I neither received it of man, neither was I taught it, but by the revelation of Jesus Christ. (Gal. 1:11–12)

In what has gone before this, Paul had pronounced an *anathema* upon anyone who tampered with the gospel as it originally came to the Galatians. In what follows, he gives a detailed description of his journeys in order to show that he did not "get his gospel" at secondhand from men. But here he tells what his gospel is not, and what it is.

Paul has already told them that the gospel he had preached to them (the gospel which was the benchmark of the truth) concerned how God would deliver sinners from "this present evil world" (v. 4). This gospel that Paul preached was not "after man" (v. 11). The original here is *kata anthropon*—according to man. That which is according *to* man is also in accordance *with* man. A man-made gospel will always cut with the fleshly grain, and will always flatter in a way that the divine gospel will not. This flattery usually takes one of two forms—either indulgence or severity. Alien to the mind of the flesh is anything like *grace*. And what grace! And this leads to the next issue.

Paul says he did not receive this gospel from man. He did not learn it in a classroom in seminary somewhere. Rather, he received it by the revelation of Jesus Christ. The Greek word here for revelation is *apocalypse*, or unveiling. How did Paul come to possess this gospel? He received it in a revelation of Jesus Christ. When we look in Scripture for an account of this, we see that it was far more than mere data transfer between the mind of Christ and the mind of Paul. Paul talks about this revelation in another place, when he is giving his testimony before King Agrippa. "At midday, O king, I saw in the way a light from heaven, above the brightness of the sun, shining round about me and them which journeyed with me" (Acts 26:13). This was the unveiling, the apocalypse. He was in no way disobedient to this heavenly vision (v. 19). Jesus Christ *appeared* to him, and ordained him as a minister and as a witness (vv. 15–18). The potency of this gospel is seen in that it would open the sinners' eyes, turn them from darkness to light, and from the power of Satan to God (v. 18).

Our tendency is to think that the gospel is divine simply because God is the one who thought it up. This is true, but inadequate. The gospel is divine because through the gospel we are introduced into the divine life. If we have been baptized into Christ, Paul argues later, we have *put on Christ*. What does this mean? Union with Christ is what enables us to be drawn into the fellowship that has always existed between the Father, Son, and Holy Spirit.

The grace of God is *not* "I forgive your sins. Run along." The grace of God is seen in this: "I forgive your sins. Enter in." Enter into what? The answer given in the divine gospel is entry into the divine life: "And this is the record, that God hath given to us eternal life, *and this life is in his Son*. He that hath the Son hath life; and he that hath not the Son of God hath not life" (1 John 5:11–12).

This being the case, what do we have to be thankful for? We overflow with thanks because we not only assemble *before* the Lord, we also are permitted to assemble *in* the Lord. In Christ, we have all the treasures of the divine life. We not only stagger to think of this, we stagger if we merely *begin* to think about it. This is Paul's prayer, that the eyes of our understanding would be enlightened, that we might know the hope of his calling, and what are the riches of the glory of his inheritance in the saints (Eph. 1:18).

THE CONVERSION OF SAUL

We have all heard about the conversion of Saul on the road to Damascus. But what exactly was he converted *from*? The answer to this question is highly significant, and we need to get it right if we are to understand the rest of this epistle.

> For ye have heard of my conversation in time past in the Jews' religion, how that beyond measure I perse-cuted the church of God, and wasted it: and profited in the Jews' religion above many my equals in mine own nation, being more exceedingly zealous of the tradi-tions of my fathers. (Gal. 1:13–14)

When Paul had first preached to the Galatians, he also had told them about his previous life before he had encountered Christ. He refers to that important fact here again. He had told them about his previous "conversation," which is an older English expression for "manner of life." Paul mentions "Judaism" twice in these two verses. He refers to it as an objective set of beliefs, as a religion distinct from the Church of God, and as one with an identifiable body of belief, which he here identifies as the tradition of his fathers. This Judaism is *not* to be understood as the faith of those in the old covenant who looked forward to the coming of the Messiah in true and genuine faith. Mary and Joseph, Anna, Simeon, John the Baptist, et al. were *not* members of this "Judaism."

A few chapters later, Paul makes this point as bluntly as such a point can be made (4:21–26). Those who desired to be "under the law" were in effect Ishmaelites. Proud of their descent from the free woman, they were actually sons of Hagar, sons of a slave woman, and not true sons of Abraham. But remember that it was the kind of mistake that was easy *for a certain kind of heart* to make. The two women lived in the same place.

Those born "after the flesh" will always persecute the sons of the free woman (4:29). Just as Ishmael taunted Isaac, so the deep antipathy continues down to the present. This, and this only, is what accounts for Paul's savagery against the Church of God. He says this strongly in two ways. First, he not only persecuted the Church of God, but he did so "beyond measure" (v. 13). The word here is *hyperbolen*, which could be rendered by our idiom "over the top." His persecution was precisely not measured, but rather blind and irrational. He says this another way when he says the result of his attacks was that the Church was destroyed or wasted. The only other time this word is used besides in this chapter (vv. 13, 23) is in Acts 9:21, when people are talking about Saul's assault on the Church. And remember the word Luke used to describe how Paul "savaged" or "mauled" the Church (Acts 8:3; 9:1). This was no ecclesiastical misunderstanding, no mere verbal skirmish over covenantal boundary markers. Paul was an evil, wicked, and unconverted man. He was an insolent, blaspheming man (1 Tim. 1:13).

But it is not enough just to be "against" something. Paul was certainly that, but men are created in such a way as to *need* a god in their system, and their god cannot be silent. It is not enough to be against the true God. An idol is logically necessary. And the idol must speak and direct those who worship him. In this case, the god was Judaism, and this god spoke through the tradition of the fathers. These traditions had the effect of supplanting the Word of God (and this is precisely the effect they were *intended* to have). Idols are not shy about expressing their will and desire. And what did Jesus teach us about the force of autonomous tradition in Mark 7:9? Now remember that human tradition is necessary, but it is never a necessary *god*. It is necessary, in fact, for our traditions to be kept in their appropriate place.

This is important on two levels. The first is that as part of what is called a "new perspective on Paul" some scholars today want to represent the pre-Christian Saul as a *faithful* representative of Old Testament religion. The reasons for this vary, but the results of thinking this way are consistently destructive. Saul's conversion was *not* simply a

matter of understanding the transition to a new economy
of salvation that acknowledged Jesus as the Messiah. Much
more was involved than that. Scripture teaches that Saul
was not like the Bereans at all (Acts 17:11). He had to be
converted, not convinced (1 Tim. 1:15–16).

The second reason is this. We must learn to maintain balance as we seek to live our lives as faithful members of the
new covenant. We reject every form of morbid introspec-
tion, but the biblical alternative to this is *not* a glib covenant presumption. The dividing line between sons of Sarah
and sons of Hagar is never works, but always faith. And this
means that true sons and daughters of the covenant will
always look to Christ.

HOW MANY TRIPS TO JERUSALEM?

The apostle Paul now gives a detailed account of his trips
to Jerusalem. This was not important in itself, but it had
become important because of the false accusations that had
been leveled at him.

> But when it pleased God, who separated me from my
> mother's womb, and called me by his grace, To reveal
> his Son in me, that I might preach him among the
> heathen; immediately I conferred not with flesh and
> blood: Neither went I up to Jerusalem to them which
> were apostles before me; but I went into Arabia, and
> returned again unto Damascus. Then after three years I
> went up to Jerusalem to see Peter, and abode with him
> fifteen days. But other of the apostles saw I none, save

James the Lord's brother. Now the things which I write
unto you, behold, before God, I lie not. Afterwards
I came into the regions of Syria and Cilicia; And was
unknown by face unto the churches of Judaea which
were in Christ: But they had heard only, That he which
persecuted us in times past now preacheth the faith
which once he destroyed. And they glorified God in me.
(Gal. 1:15–24)

The conversion of Saul was not an afterthought on the
part of God. Saul was elect from before the foundation of
the world, and he had been set apart for his apostleship
from the time he was in his mother's womb (v. 15). At that
moment on the Damascus road, Saul was effectually called
by the grace of God. At the same time, Jesus Christ was
revealed *in* Saul, in order that he might become an apostolic
preacher to the Gentiles (v. 16).

The false teacher or teachers at Galatia were intimating
that Saul was instructed in the rudiments of the Christian
faith by the other apostles, which would make him (at best)
a second-tier apostle. His adversaries could then claim that
as a pupil, he was not a very good one. *They*, in fact, had
gotten the lessons right. This is why Paul had to emphasize
that he had *not* conferred with flesh and blood (v. 16). Not
only that, but he did not even *go* to Jerusalem until three
years *later* (vv. 17–18). When he finally got around to going
to Jerusalem, he was there for the very short space of fifteen
days—hardly time to get a seminary education (v. 18).

The only other person ranked among the apostles that
he saw there was James, the brother of the Lord. This is

interesting because James was not numbered among the Twelve, and was apparently not a believer in Jesus until after the resurrection (John 7:5; 1 Cor. 15:7; Acts 1:14). Nevertheless, he came to faith and soon assumed a position of authority in the Jerusalem church (Acts 12:17). Paul acknowledges him as a pillar (2:9) and one of some repute (2:6), and here in this place seems to number him among the apostles. But his acquaintance with James was first made during that two weeks.

So Paul was in Damascus/Arabia/Damascus for three years (Acts 9:19ff; 2 Cor. 11:32–33). He then came to Jerusalem for just over two weeks, and the visit was cut short by an attempt on his life (Acts 9:29). He then went to Tarsus (in Cilicia) for ten years, after which Barnabas brought him down to Antioch (in Syria) for a year. So then, fourteen years after his conversion, he went to Jerusalem for the *second* time (Gal. 2:1).

Paul mentions his time in Syria and Cilicia here in passing (v. 21). The churches of Judea that were in Christ did not know him (v. 22)—he had spent virtually no time there. They of course had heard of him, but what they heard was simply that a former persecutor had turned preacher (v. 23). They gave glory to God for this (v. 23), which incidentally was not something that the false teachers in Galatia were prepared to do.

Now let us take this back to verse 20. There Paul swears an oath before God. He says that this account of his trips to Jerusalem was *absolutely* accurate—so help him God. Given this vow, it is nothing short of astounding that there are conservative Bible scholars who identify the Jerusalem visit coming up in Galatians 2 with the Jerusalem Council visit of Acts 15. This overlooks the famine relief visit (Acts 11:27–30), and would make Paul's vow false. Not only that, but it is a vow that is part of inspired Scripture—which means the Holy Spirit inspired a lie, which is obviously problematic and therefore false. Not only is this unworthy of Paul and Scripture, it would also be counter-productive for him to take an oath that would give significant leverage to the false teachers in Galatia when they showed that his vow was clearly false since he had spent a significant amount of time with the apostles at an unmentioned famine relief visit.

Not only that, but it ignores the inexplicable neglect of any reference to the decisions of the council in Galatians. If Galatians was written after the Jerusalem Council, then what was Paul thinking by not mentioning it? Why does he act in this book as though the question were unsettled, when in fact the first great council of the church had settled it?

We can also see here a biblical pattern for responding to false reports. First, Paul was a man of godly character, *known* to the Galatians. Second, *because* of this he was attacked. Third, he responds with a vow—firmly attached to information that could be independently confirmed.

All things in Scripture are written for our instruction, for our profit. It is truly unfortunate, but many well-intentioned Christians do not understand these principles. There is little doubt they would reject Paul's argument as well—if it were not in the Bible.

GALATIANS 2

FALSE BROTHERS

In the Christian faith, particular events, schedules, persons, and conversations *matter*. They matter because we are talking about God's intervention in *history*. The gospel is not a detached and abstracted affair—a set of timeless truths in the heavenlies. Particularity matters a great deal.

> Then fourteen years after I went up again to Jerusalem with Barnabas, and took Titus with me also. And I went up by revelation, and communicated unto them that gospel which I preach among the Gentiles, but privately to them which were of reputation, lest by any means I should run, or had run, in vain. But neither Titus, who was with me, being a Greek, was compelled

to be circumcised: And that because of false brethren
unawares brought in, who came in privily to spy out our
liberty which we have in Christ Jesus, that they might
bring us into bondage: To whom we gave place by subjection, no, not for an hour; that the truth of the gospel
might continue with you. (Gal. 2:1–5)

Paul has been very emphatic about how many times
he has been to Jerusalem (1:20). This visit to Jerusalem
described in the second chapter of Galatians must therefore
be the famine relief visit described in Acts 11. Let us consider how the two visits line up.

And in these days came prophets from Jerusalem
unto Antioch. And there stood up one of them named
Agabus, and signified by the Spirit that there should be
great dearth throughout all the world: which came to
pass in the days of Claudius Caesar. Then the disciples,
every man according to his ability, determined to send
relief unto the brethren which dwelt in Judaea: Which
also they did, and sent it to the elders by the hands of
Barnabas and Saul. (Acts 11:27–30)

First, St. Paul identifies the two visits. Second, both visits were in response to a revelation (Gal. 2:2; Acts 11:28).
Third, both visits were for the sake of the poor (Acts 11:29;
Gal. 2:10). Fourth, Paul took Barnabas on both trips (Acts
11:30; Gal. 2:1). Fifth, Paul does not mention the decision of
the Jerusalem Council in the book of Galatians, which would
be inexplicable if the council had already decided in his favor.

The apostle Paul tells us something about the Acts 11 visit that we do not learn from Acts, which is that Paul met with the leaders (those who were "of reputation") in the Jerusalem church (and he did so privately) in order to set out his gospel before them, the gospel he preached to the Gentiles. He did this because he was afraid that the Jerusalem leaders might undo his work, and all his labors would have been in vain. Fortunately, this did not happen—the leaders of the Jerusalem church stood fast in the standards of grace.

Titus was the test case. He was a Greek and therefore was not circumcised. He accompanied Paul and Barnabas on this trip, and he was received as a brother (just the way he was) by the Jerusalem leaders. And this was not because they did not notice he was Greek. Certain men had demanded that Titus be compelled to accept circumcision, Paul's party refused to accommodate them, even for a minute, *and the Jerusalem leaders sided with Paul.*

Now what are we to make of this category, "false brethren"? These men were not outliers in the Jerusalem church. Their baptismal papers were in good order, they had access to the inner councils of the apostles and elders and were no doubt included as elders among them. Yet Paul calls them false brothers. The objectivity of the covenant means that these men were objectively brothers, in the same sense that an unfaithful husband is truly a husband. But an unfaithful husband is not a true husband in that he is false to his vows and his covenant obligations. It is the same kind of thing here. If a betrayed wife says to her husband, "You are a false husband" and he responds with, "That means that I had no true vows to break," this means he is just compounding his wickedness. We all know how to distinguish the words *true* and *false* easily and readily—until we get to the covenant of grace. But we really must learn to grow up.

Paul knew how to bend for the sake of the weaker brother. He knew how to teach us how to bend for the sake of the weaker brother. We are not to stumble one another over debatable issues (Rom. 14; 1 Cor. 8). At the same time, he could be the most *inflexible* of men when the principles central to the gospel were at stake (Col. 2:16). Further, he required the same kind of flexibility and inflexibility from us, as we imitate him. Is the gospel under assault in our day? Always and everywhere. What are we to do? Stand fast.

MEN FROM JAMES

The ancient church, like the modern church, was not without its tensions and differences. Those tensions existed even among the apostles, and how they were addressed gives us direction and guidance.

> But of these who seemed to be somewhat, (whatsoever they were, it maketh no matter to me: God accepteth no man's person:) for they who seemed to be somewhat in conference added nothing to me: But contrariwise, when they saw that the gospel of the uncircumcision was committed unto me, as the gospel of the circumcision was unto Peter; (For he that wrought effectually in Peter to the apostleship of the circumcision, the same was mighty in me toward the Gentiles:) And when James, Cephas, and John, who seemed to be pillars,

perceived the grace that was given unto me, they gave
to me and Barnabas the right hands of fellowship; that
we should go unto the heathen, and they unto the circumcision. Only they would that we should remember
the poor; the same which I also was forward to do.
(Gal. 2:6–10)

St. Paul has no difficulty with apostolic authority at all.
He claims it for himself, and he is particularly zealous to
honor the work of another man's foundation. At the same
time, he *does* have difficulty with those who render honor to
those in true authority, but who do so in a wrong way. Paul
is here describing some tense negotiations at the time of the
famine relief visit. We have already seen that false brothers
had insinuated themselves into the councils of the leaders
at Jerusalem, just described, and certain "men from James"
had caused an earlier fracas at Antioch (Gal. 2:12). This
famine relief "summit" did not solve this problem either, for
later on, the controversy at Antioch was created by certain
"men from Judea" (Acts 15:1). The council itself shows that
they exceeded their authority; the controversy itself shows
that the circle of James was infiltrated by false brothers.

So keep in mind what Paul said in the first chapter—"if
we or an angel from heaven." This is the context in which
he slights the *human* authority of the leaders at Jerusalem.
This is the meaning of those "who seemed to be somewhat,"
and who "seemed to be pillars." The gospel outranks each
apostle individually, and all of them collectively. This was
important to emphasize since there were many at Jerusalem who looked to James for all the wrong reasons.

Paul testifies that the result of this secret summit was successful. These leaders at Jerusalem saw and acknowledged that Paul was entrusted with the gospel to the Gentiles, in just the same way that gospel to the Jews had been entrusted to Peter (v. 7). Not only so, but God had worked powerfully in each of them in their respective realms of ministry (v. 8). When all these men—James, Cephas, and John—saw the grace that had been bestowed upon Paul, they extended to him the right hand of fellowship. They were not working at odds with one another, although it must still be emphasized that *some of their followers were* working at odds with one another.

I am not accustomed to quoting John Dewey favorably, but he once said something well worth repeating again: "Lord, deliver me from my disciples!" The followers of Paul have often not represented him well, and have veered off toward antinomianism. The followers of James have often not represented him well either, and have veered off toward legalism. What does this do to Romans and James? Nothing—they are both the inspired Word of God. Paul and James shook hands with one another, while some of their ostensible followers cannot do so.

One result of the summit was that the Jerusalem leaders asked that Paul would continue to remember the poor. But of course, this was during the famine relief visit of Acts 11, so that was exactly why Paul had come with Barnabas to Jerusalem in the first place. This reveals something to us about the nature of conflict or tension. Frequently, we find just this problem—what someone is doing, or even excelling at doing, is ignored and overlooked, and they are solemnly urged to correct the deficiency, or to guard against it. Fish are urged to remain wet, and birds are exhorted to remember the importance of flying. Paul is apparently just a tad exasperated.

The Bible requires us to honor and obey those who are in spiritual leadership over us (Heb. 13:7, 17). At the same time, it requires us also to remember that they partake of our common sinful maladies, and they are quite capable of disgracing their ministries and themselves. But this does not require an attitude of suspicion, but rather of humble prayer, the right kind of obedience, the right kind of honor—not like that which was rendered to James by the false brothers.

THE FAITH OF JESUS

We now come to a discussion of a showdown between Peter and Paul at Antioch. The confrontation, the reasons for it, and the solution to it are all filled with instruction for us.

> But when Peter was come to Antioch, I withstood him to the face, because he was to be blamed. For before that certain came from James, he did eat with the Gentiles: but when they were come, he withdrew and separated himself, fearing them which were of the circumcision . . . . (Gal. 2:11–21)

Paul now recounts a problem he had with Peter at Antioch, and this happened because Peter was to be blamed (v. 11). Peter had been eating together with Gentiles, but when men from James came to Antioch, he withdrew because he

was afraid of "the circumcision party" (v. 12). This stum-
bled other believing Jews into *hypocrisy*, even including
Barnabas (v. 13). When Paul saw they were not walking in
accordance with the Gospel, he asked them an unanswer-
able question. If Jews do not have to live like Jews, then why
do Gentiles have to live like Jews (v. 14)?

Paul then explains this. Jews by nature, and not Gentile
sinners (v. 15), know that we are justified by the faith of
Christ and not by the works of the law (v. 16). But does the
admission of a need for justification from sin make God a
minister of sin (v. 17)? Absolutely not. Renovation presup-
poses destruction, but that is no argument against renovat-
ing (v. 18). Through the law we die to the law so that we
might live before God (v. 19). We are crucified with Christ,
and this makes us participants in both His death and resurrection (v. 20). This is in no way a frustration of grace
because Christ cannot have died in vain (v. 21).

So what was the nature of this hypocrisy that Peter had
fallen into? We must be very careful here, because Peter's
hypocrisy was a mirror-image hypocrisy. Most hypocrisy is
public righteousness and private sin. This was the hypocrisy
of the Pharisees—outside was a beautiful tomb and inside
were dead men's bones. But Peter (and Barnabas, and other
Jews at Antioch) had reversed this. They were privately
orthodox and godly and publicly sinful. Peter held to the
proposition of justification by faith throughout this entire
controversy. But he denied that proposition by his *actions*
when he refused table fellowship with fellow Christians.
Paul calls this hypocrisy (v. 12), and he says that it is not
walking uprightly in the truth of the gospel (v. 14).

Pay close attention. What should we call it when a sect refuses to share communion with other Christian churches? Paul calls it hypocrisy, and a functional denial of justification by faith alone. The irony is that many sects refuse to share communion because of how tightly they hold to justification by faith alone. This simply gives us a double layer of hypocrisy, and a remarkable denial of justification through their restrictions on table fellowship.

What is meant by "the faith of Jesus Christ"? In verse 16, we find a striking phrase (which is repeated twice). We know that men are not justified by the works of Judaic law-keeping, but "by the faith of Jesus Christ." We have believed in Jesus "that we might be justified by the faith of Christ." Now is this *our* faith, or is it Jesus' faith? Our faith is mentioned, but our believing in Jesus is *so that* we might be justified by the faith of Jesus.

This is in contrast to being justified "by the works of the law." The reason for that is because "for by the works of the law shall no flesh be justified." By the works of the law everybody goes to hell. Note well, then, that our justification depends on the faith of Jesus, Jesus believing. Our faith is the instrument which unites us with Christ, and it is in *union with Christ* (and thereby with His faith) that we find our justification. In the imputation of the active and passive obedience of Christ to us, we do not just receive "His actions." Everything Jesus said and did is imputed to us, along with His motives for saying and doing them. The imputation of Christ's righteousness to us cannot be accomplished unless His faith is imputed to us as well—because Christ's righteousness was not independent of His faith.

For these reasons I take it as the objective faith *of* Jesus Christ, which becomes ours through faith *in* Jesus.

But there are some odd objections. In order to be united with Christ in His death and resurrection, both Jews and Gentiles had to acknowledge that they were sinners. We are united with sin on the cross so that sin might there die, and that we might be subsequently raised. Does this promote sin (v. 17)? Of course not. Always remember the importance of resurrection; we include both destruction *and* rebuilding (v. 18). The law kills and we are raised, together with the law (v. 19).

This is the key to understanding Paul's theology of justification. Union with Christ begins with crucifixion (v. 20). Nevertheless, life follows, *and it is the life of Christ which follows.* This life of Christ includes His faith. "The life which I now live in the flesh I live by the faith of the Son of God, who loved me, and gave himself for me." How could this frustrate the grace of God? It *is* the grace of God (v. 21). Righteousness does not come by the law. It does not come by fencing the Table. If we must fence the Table against fellow believers, then Christ died in vain (v. 21).

GALATIANS 3

FAITH ALONE, FAITH ALWAYS

The reason there is a crisis in Galatia is because the saints have given the time of day to a teacher or teachers they ought to have ignored. Paul brings this basic problem home to the Galatian believers in a very pointed way.

> O foolish Galatians, who hath bewitched you, that ye should not obey the truth, before whose eyes Jesus Christ hath been evidently set forth, crucified among you? This only would I learn of you, Received ye the Spirit by the works of the law, or by the hearing of faith? Are ye so foolish? having begun in the Spirit, are ye now made perfect by the flesh? Have ye suffered so many things in vain? if it be yet in vain. He therefore

that ministereth to you the Spirit, and worketh miracles
among you, doeth he it by the works of the law, or by
the hearing of faith? (Gal. 3:1–5)

Paul comes now to a pointed rebuke. The false teachers
have done what false teachers do. But the Galatians had
been true disciples, and Paul is extremely distraught with
them over their behavior. He begins by calling them foolish
(v. 1), and asks who had cast a spell on them—he does not
know how to account for their behavior otherwise (v. 1). It
had to be a powerful enchantment indeed, because Jesus
Christ had been plainly preached as crucified before them.

His fundamental argument, which he presses here, asks
them how they received the Spirit. How did the Spirit work
among them? Why are they even thinking about changing
to "another way"? Paul's fundamental assumption here is
that we live like Christians in the same way that we became
Christians. We receive the Spirit by faith. What makes us
think that we are to retain the Spirit by any other means
than this same faith?

A very common and dangerous assumption among Christians is that "true" Christians cannot be enticed by heresy.
Now it is true that the elect will persevere to the end, and
they will continue to hear the shepherd's voice, but it is *not*
true that this all happens with them coasting easily down-
hill into glory. Those whom God has chosen to be saved will
in fact be saved, but it does not follow from this that they
will not face obstacles to that final salvation on the way.

In the case of the Galatians, Paul had to (verbally) slap
them around—they were entertaining very dangerous

opinions, and they thought that they had every right to do this. So Paul calls them *foolish* Christians. He says their behavior could be accounted for if he postulated some kind of wizard casting spells on them. This is the nature of life prior to the resurrection; we should never forget that the Church contains many Christians capable of acting very foolishly. And there are even times when the sin is worse within the Church than outside.

Paul is warning them against the "deeper walk trap." Despite how clearly Paul has spoken on the subject here, a persistent error in the Church says that yes, you come to Jesus by grace through faith. But then, if you really want to "enter in" the deeper life, or the higher life, or the special life, you must do something else, of another nature. That something else might be speaking in tongues, receiving a mystic vision, or memorizing the Shorter Catechism. But the Scriptures teach us that we are to continue to walk in the same way we began to walk, which is by grace through faith. We have this passage; we *continue* the same, identical way we *began*. Paul also says in Colossians 2:6, "As ye have therefore received Christ Jesus the Lord, so walk ye in him." By grace through faith, from first to last. Faith alone, faith always.

Paul is clearly *arguing* his case. But as with everything else, an argument like this can only be followed in the power of the Spirit. First, he says, did you receive the Spirit by hearing with faith or by works of the law? (But the subtext here is that they could only receive Paul's argument *by faith*.) Paul then assumes that their behavior answers the question wrongly. "Are you so foolish?" he says (v. 3). If you couldn't *start* without the Spirit's work, what makes you think you can *run* without the Spirit's work? If you cannot take the first step of the marathon without the Holy Spirit, why do you want to run the marathon without the Spirit? (Subtext: if you cannot begin without the Spirit, how can you read my argument here in Galatians without the Spirit?) Their behavior is *throwing away so much good*—making their previous suffering a vanity (v. 4). He states the argument again another way. What about all the miracles the Spirit has performed in your midst? Did He do that because you all were circumcised? Or because of your faith?

The fleshly man does not understand the things of the Spirit because they are spiritually discerned: "But the natural man receiveth not the things of the Spirit of God: for they are foolishness unto him: neither can he know them, because they are spiritually discerned" (1 Cor. 2:14). We declare, we preach, we argue, we write, we plead, we point. This is just another way of saying we plow, we plant, we weed, we hoe, we water—but only God gives the increase. Believe in God, therefore, and in His Son, Jesus Christ, in the power of the Holy Spirit.

ABRAHAM AND THE GOSPEL

We come now to the glorious example of Abraham, and the apostle Paul draws much gold out of the mines of Genesis. We will be occupied with this gold for much of the remainder of the third chapter of Galatians.

> Even as Abraham believed God, and it was accounted
> to him for righteousness. Know ye therefore that

they which are of faith, the same are the children of Abraham. And the scripture, foreseeing that God would justify the heathen through faith, preached before the gospel unto Abraham, saying, In thee shall all nations be blessed. So then they which be of faith are blessed with faithful Abraham. For as many as are of the works of the law are under the curse: for it is written, Cursed is every one that continueth not in all things which are written in the book of the law to do them. But that no man is justified by the law in the sight of God, it is evident: for, The just shall live by faith. And the law is not of faith: but, The man that doeth them shall live in them. (Gal. 3:6–12)

Abraham trusted in God, and that was reckoned to him as righteousness (v. 6). And those who do the same thing that Abraham did can rightly be considered his children (v. 7). Not only this, but Scripture prophesied that this would in fact happen to the Gentiles when the gospel was declared to Abraham (v. 8). That *gospel* was put this way—through Abraham *all* the nations would be blessed. That blessing is identified as the opportunity of being blessed with Abraham (v. 9), and this is for everyone who is "of faith."

Being "of faith" is contrasted with being "of the works of the law." Those who are of faith are blessed; those who are of the Judaic works of the law are cursed (v. 10). Everyone who does not continue in the works of the law is cursed (v. 10). It is clear, Paul says, that no one is justified by law-keeping, for the just will live by faith (v. 11). The law, on the other hand, is based on *doing*, not *believing* (v. 12).

God told Abraham something, and Abraham believed *God* concerning that something. Note first that the object of Abraham's faith was God. The "carrier" of this, the thing that Abraham wound up believing, was that all nations would be blessed through him.

This is so important. The sentence is *Abraham believed God*, not *Abraham believed in Abraham believing the right way*. The Scriptures do not say here that Abraham came to understand justification by faith. It says that he believed God. The gospel, as it was declared to Abraham, was that the heathen would all be converted. *That* is the gospel. *That* is what Abraham believed. *That* is what Abraham saw. As Jesus told the Jews, "Your father Abraham rejoiced to see my day: and he saw *it*, and was glad" (John 8:56).

So *how* do the heathen partake? The contrast is between those who are "of faith" and those who are "of the works of the law." But we must be very careful here. The contrast is not between the grace of "not having to do" and the work of having to do. This is backward. The contrast is between the grace of "getting to do" and the condemnation of "not being able to do."

Why are men never justified by the works of the law? It is not because they do them, only to discover it is no good to do them like that. The reason law-keeping doesn't work is because men don't do it. Those who are of the works of the law are under a curse because—cursed is everyone *that continues not . . .* Remember that we are under grace, not under law. Therefore sin is no longer our master (Rom. 6:14).

No man is justified by law. The just shall live by faith. The context of this argument is that no man is justified by keeping the works of law in a Mosaic context. But if we are spiritually wise, we will apply this central biblical principle to *every* form of "law-keeping." Men are summoned to believe God, and not to seek to justify themselves through circumcision, Passover-keeping, monkish zeal, or by affirming *sola fide*. Affirming *sola fide* as a means of justifying oneself is a denial of *sola fide*.

What is the mark of faith? Jump to the end of this chapter. We will consider this in greater detail later, but what distinguishes these Gentiles who have believed from others who have not (Gal. 3:27–29)? We have to remember two things. First, baptism is the mark of this promise to all nations, and not the nationally limited mark of circumcision. True faith was no more visible to the naked eye in the first century than it is today. Second, those who are so baptized need to remember the solemn warnings that Paul gave to baptized Gentiles over against circumcised Jews. He commanded them not to make the same mistake the Jews had made. We do not support the root; the root supports us (Rom. 11:19–22). The formal mark of the Christian is water baptism (Gal. 3:27), which nourishes the fruit of the Spirit (Gal. 5:22-23), which is the mark that indicates someone has the root of the matter in him (John 13:35, Mark 4:6).

PROMISE BEFORE LAW

We have learned that those who are under the law are under a curse. This is because being under the law does not mean that one keeps the law; rather, it means that one does not keep it, and is therefore under condemnation. And make no mistake—all have sinned in this way. How can sinful men be delivered from this state of condemnation?

> Christ hath redeemed us from the curse of the law, being made a curse for us: for it is written, Cursed is every one that hangeth on a tree: That the blessing of Abraham might come on the Gentiles through Jesus Christ; that we might receive the promise of the Spirit through faith. Brethren, I speak after the manner of men; Though it be but a man's covenant, yet if it be confirmed, no man disannulleth, or addeth thereto. Now to Abraham and his seed were the promises made. He saith not, And to seeds, as of many; but as of one, And to thy seed, which is Christ. And this I say, that the covenant, that was confirmed before of God in Christ, the law, which was four hundred and thirty years after, cannot disannul, that it should make the promise of none effect. For if the inheritance be of the law, it is no more of promise: but God gave it to Abraham by promise. (Gal. 3:13–18)

We are redeemed from this curse of ours because Christ became a curse in our stead. The Bible pronounces a curse upon everyone hanged on a tree, and Christ was in fact hanged on a tree (v. 13). He did this in order that the blessing of Abraham might come upon the Gentiles, that is, the promise of the Spirit through faith (v. 14). Using a human illustration, Paul says that even a man-made covenant is not altered after the fact (v. 15). Now the promise was made to Abraham and his seed, meaning Christ (v. 16). The Mosaic law came centuries after the promise (to the Gentiles) was confirmed in Christ (v. 17). The law, which came later, was therefore not the ordained instrument through which the promise was to be fulfilled (v. 18).

In this passage, Paul is insisting that the promise to Christ in Abraham was foundational, and that the law was added *later*, for supplementary reasons. The law was therefore an instrument that was subordinate to the promise. The promise was not subordinate to the law. Such theological contextualization is crucial—how we answer such questions will determine whether we be joyful Christians or pious prunes.

Let's push it further back. Unfortunately, many Christians have gone back past Abraham, back to Adam, in order to advance their understanding of the "covenant of works" that God had with Adam. In this view, grace only comes in after the Fall. God *did* make a covenant of works with Adam in the garden, a covenant which was dependent upon Adam's obedience. But if Adam had faithfully obeyed, it would have been necessary for him to thank God for it—it would have been all of grace.

Note what a denial of this does to Paul's argument here—it makes a hash of it. Paul has impressed upon us that we need to understand that the promise came 430 years before the law. And to this, many contemporary theologians reply, "Yes, but the law in another form was two thousand years before *that*." So the law has foundational priority after all. In their defense, this is done because they want us to be saved by the second Adam's "works," and so we must be lost by the failure of the first Adam to "work." But this misconstrues (almost completely) the nature of grace. If the first

Adam had not fallen, would he have rendered thanks to God *for His grace*? When the second Adam faithfully stood the test, did *He* not do so? "In the midst of the congregation will I praise thee" (Ps. 22:22). For *what*?

So the promise was made to the seed, that is, to Christ, and so the fulfillment of the promise is available to the "seeds" of Abraham, that is, to everyone who has faith in Christ. Paul is not arguing from the grammar to Christ; he is arguing from Christ to the grammar. This glorious promise is only possible in Christ, and so therefore the seed in Genesis had to be referring to Him. Keep in mind the fact that the word *seed* can be either singular or plural.

Christ became a curse for us. The promise of blessing for the Gentiles was given to Abraham and to his seed. And yet, all Abraham's natural seed had come under the condemnation of the law through not keeping it. So far were they from bringing covenant blessings to the sons of Adam, they were actually dragging Adamic disobedience into the line of Abraham. With their Judaic distortions, the life preserver became an anvil. This is why the seed of Abraham in the promise *had* to be talking about Christ—otherwise the promise could not be fulfilled at all. Jews and Gentiles, natural sons of Adam, were both under condemnation.

In order to be free, one had to be a child of the promise. But one could not be a child of the promise without also being a child of the great transaction. Christ became a curse for us on the tree so that in Him we might become the righteousness of God (2 Cor. 5:20). Christ takes our curse, and we take His blessing. We are cursed in Him, and we are blessed in Him. We are crucified in Him, and we are raised in Him.

MORE ON PROMISE AND LAW

If our salvation is based on promise, not on law, then what
is the law for?

> Wherefore then serveth the law? It was added because
> of transgressions, till the seed should come to whom the
> promise was made; and it was ordained by angels in the
> hand of a mediator. Now a mediator is not a mediator of
> one, but God is one. Is the law then against the promises
> of God? God forbid: for if there had been a law given
> which could have given life, verily righteousness should
> have been by the law. But the scripture hath concluded
> all under sin, that the promise by faith of Jesus Christ
> might be given to them that believe. But before faith
> came, we were kept under the law, shut up unto the
> faith which should afterwards be revealed. Wherefore
> the law was our schoolmaster to bring us unto Christ,
> that we might be justified by faith. But after that faith
> is come, we are no longer under a schoolmaster. For ye
> are all the children of God by faith in Christ Jesus. For
> as many of you as have been baptized into Christ have
> put on Christ. There is neither Jew nor Greek, there is
> neither bond nor free, there is neither male nor female:
> for ye are all one in Christ Jesus. And if ye be Christ's,
> then are ye Abraham's seed, and heirs according to the
> promise. (Gal. 3:19–29)

What is based on the law? What role does it have (v. 19)?
A reasonable question—the law was added for transgression until the promised seed should come. This law was

mediated, but this means that "the Mosaic law" is not internal to the Trinity *the same way the promise is* (v. 20).[1] Are
the law and promise at odds then? Not at all—if law were
trying to do what the promise did, it would have succeeded
(v. 21). The law enrolled us all in the schoolhouse of sin
so that the promise would bring to graduation those who
believe (v. 22). We were kept under the law until the faith
(the promise) should be revealed (v. 23). The law was our
pedagogue to bring us to Christ (v. 24). But once we have
graduated and grown, the pedagogue is no longer needed
(v. 25). So all, Jew and Gentile, are children of God through
faith in Christ (v. 26). You do not need to be circumcised if
you have been baptized; if you are baptized, you have put on
Christ (v. 27). And this union in Christ creates true equality
(v. 28). And you are Christ's; you are also Abraham's, and
therefore an heir (v. 29).

So here is the point of the law. In historical theology, we
often point to the three uses of the law. This distinction is
quite helpful, as far as it goes. One use is to restrain evil
men (1 Tim. 1:8–11), another use is prepare the individual
for salvation (Rom. 3:20; 5:20), and a third use is that of
informing Christians what love actually looks like in action
(Rom. 13:8–10). But there is another important use of the
law, a use that corresponds to preparing an individual for
salvation. This is the role of preparing the *world* for salvation, and that is what we find here. Note that Paul is arguing
that the law was given until the seed should come. He is not
referring to the moment the seed "comes into the individual

---

1. This is a reference to an *ad intra* covenant of redemption between the
Father and the Son.

heart." He is speaking of the time when the seed comes into the *world*.

Then we have the puzzling phrase "God is one." This passage is obscure, and it vexes the commentators greatly. After offering all appropriate qualifications, this is how I understand it. When we see Paul's description of the law here, we see why he emphasizes that it was mediated. God was *here* and the sinful people to be redeemed were over *there*, and the law was mediated between them. But God is one and does not need a mediating agent within Him. This meant that the Mosaic law did not rise to the status (so to speak) of a divine attribute. But our salvation is based on the very nature of God, and Paul has told us that this foundation is the promise. The promise does not need an external mediator. That promise is therefore contained within the triune life, and when we are united to Christ, we are united to that living promise.

If you are baptized, you have been baptized into Christ. Therefore, Paul argues, act like it. Now this is the hinge of the argument in Galatians. Why do Gentiles not need to be circumcised? They do not need to be circumcised because baptism marks them out as belonging to Christ. And if they are Christ's, they are Abraham's. And if they are Abraham's, then they are heirs *and therefore do not need to be circumcised.*

In Christ, all barriers to fellowship are dissolved. No longer is it possible to say that I can have nothing to do with you "because you belong to the wrong caste." The three possible barriers to fellowship that Paul mentions here are racial and cultural, social, and sexual. And we may add more of our own—indeed, obedience requires it. We may not withhold fellowship based on income, race, manners, age, or Vietnam-era veteran status. This should remind us: we do not object to the diversity crowd because they want to make bricks. We object to them because they want to make bricks without straw and, in some cases, without clay.

GALATIANS 4

A BILLIONAIRE IN THE HIGH CHAIR

We continue our discussion of the relationship of the old Israel and the new Israel. And in making the obvious comparisons, Paul changes the figure slightly.

> Now I say, That the heir, as long as he is a child, differeth nothing from a servant, though he be lord of all; But is under tutors and governors until the time appointed of the father. Even so we, when we were children, were in bondage under the elements of the world: But when the fulness of the time was come, God sent forth his Son, made of a woman, made under the law, To redeem them that were under the law, that we might receive the adoption of sons. And because ye are

sons, God hath sent forth the Spirit of his Son into your
hearts, crying, Abba, Father. Wherefore thou art no
more a servant, but a son; and if a son, then an heir of
God through Christ. (Gal. 4:1–7)

In the last chapter, Paul said that Israel was under the
care of the law, under the care of a pedagogue. Here he
modifies the point slightly. The heir, when he is little, is
bossed around just like a servant (v. 1). In fact, he might be
bossed around *more* than a servant is. The servant might
actually be the one doing the bossing. He is under the care
of pedagogues, tutors, and governors during the time of his
minority (v. 2). And Paul then refers to the infancy of the
world. Even so, we were in bondage to the elements (*stoichea*) of the world (v. 3). But when the right time in history
arrived, God sent His Son, born of a woman, born under the
law (v. 4). God did this to make it possible for us to leave our
minority and enter into our full adoption as sons (v. 5). And
because you (Gentiles) are sons (also), God has given you
His Spirit (v. 6). And so you Gentiles are no longer servants,
but sons, and not only sons, but grown-up sons. This means
you Gentiles are heirs (v. 7).

A billionaire in a high chair has a good deal of money but
has no real access to it. And a nanny whose net worth is a
good deal less than his may be completely in charge of him.
But this condition is temporary. The nanny and the school-
teacher and the tutor are all helping him to grow to maturity. Now what the Judaizers wanted, to continue with the
illustration, was for a billionaire's nanny of twenty years to
march up into his corporate boardroom and insist that he

take a nap right now. But he has grown up now and does not have to do these things. A servant who thought she had this kind of authority (because she had something like it once) is utterly confused about the nature of maturity and time.

But remember also that the billionaire, while he does not have to take his nap, does have to remember that two plus two equals four, just like his childhood teacher taught him, and that a good night's rest is important. The law does not go away, but the nanny forms of it *do* go away.

What is assumed in the illustration? This illustration of Paul's does much the same thing that his illustration of the olive tree in Romans 11 does—it demonstrates the essential continuity of the Old Testament people of God and the New Testament people of God. The old Israel has become the new Israel. At the same time, the word *new* here refers to much more than a little touch-up paint. The *new* is the *new* of resurrection. The continuity is that the body that is raised is the body that was killed. Some of the continuity folks want to preserve continuity by denying death. Some of the discontinuity folks want to achieve newness through the fiat creation of a new entity, *ex nihilo*.

The apostle says here that the Jews were under bondage to the *stoichea*, the basic principles of the old world, the world that came to an end in Christ. We will discuss this further shortly. The Gentiles were the servants in this old world. But when just the right time in world history came, God sent His Son into the world *in order to accomplish the crucifixion and resurrection of that entire order*. He did this in order to make all things new; He did this to redeem us from the curse of the law. He has included the Gentiles with

His Spirit, and this means that we, together with the Jews, can cry out, "Abba."

And notice Paul's shift of pronouns here. Through the first part of this, he speaks of *we*, referring to *we Jews*. Up through verse 5, Paul is talking about the Jews, who were the underage billionaire. The Gentiles were the servants. But now the sons have entered their majority (receiving the adoption as sons), and the servants have also been adopted as sons. And both kinds of sons have all grown up.

This was the situation when the conflict in Galatia erupted. Some of the billionaire Jews had now come to Galatia and were telling the newly adopted billionaire Gentiles that *they* had an advantage as Jews. "Because *we* grew up in this house, *we* took naps every afternoon. If you really want to be a billionaire, you should start taking naps too."

THE OLD ELEMENTS AND THE NEW CHRISTIAN AEON

In this epistle to the Galatians, not only do we have a contrast between the old Israel and the new, we also have a contrast between the old world and the new, between the old heavens and the old earth, and the new heavens and the new earth.

> Howbeit then, when ye knew not God, ye did service unto them which by nature are no gods. But now, after that ye have known God, or rather are known of God, how turn ye again to the weak and beggarly elements, whereunto ye desire again to be in bondage? Ye observe

days, and months, and times, and years. I am afraid of
you, lest I have bestowed upon you labour in vain. (Gal.
4:8–11)

Back when the Gentiles did not know God, they offered
service or worshipful obedience to entities which by nature
were not true gods (v. 8). But now these Gentiles know God,
or rather, Paul says, correcting himself, are known *by* God.
How is it then that they turn back to bondage? Why do they
go back to the *stoichea*, those weak and beggarly elements
(v. 9)? And how was this turning back manifested? It was
manifested through a zeal for days, months, times, and
years—all ways of cleaning the outside of the cup (v. 10).
Paul is fearful over them, afraid that all his work with them
was vanity (v. 11).

He is talking about the old world, constituted of Jew and
Gentile. But the old order of things has passed away. That
includes the witness God had established for Himself in that
old order, which was the old Israel. In the old order, the
Gentiles used to be in bondage to the elementals, and the
Jews were in the bondage of having to learn their lessons.
In that old order, the Jews were the elect people of God, but
now that Gentiles have been included in the household of
faith in the new world, for those Gentiles to go back to the
godly old order is still going back to the old order.

The Gentile knowledge of God is the result of the grace
of God. But if we speak this way too readily, we can come
to forget that it is in fact grace. So we remind ourselves that
the Gentiles were known by God first, and as a result they
came to know Him.

But what were these weak and beggarly elements? This idea of the stoichea was common in the ancient world. Plato, Aristotle, and the Stoics all shared this view of the cosmos as made up of earth, air, water, and fire. Aristotle added the possible fifth element of ether. Paul says that these things are by nature not gods. He is implying, further, that for residents of the new order to return to the Mosaic code, which was by nature from God, was tantamount to returning to the pagan idolatry that was pervasive in the ancient world also. Note also that the stoichea are fundamental to the philosophy of the ancients. Philosophy and cosmology are not separable. There is one use of the word in the New Testament where it refers to the basic principles of Christian teaching (Heb. 5:12). Here in Galatians the word refers to the rudiments of the old world. In Colossians (2:8, 20), it refers to the rudiments of the world, in opposition to Christ, of which pagan philosophy was a natural expression. In Christ, we are dead to the stoichea in this sense. In 2 Peter 3:10–12, stoichea refers to that old heaven and earth that was to be replaced by the new heavens and new earth. The parallel between this passage and Jude (17–19) shows us that this great transition occurred in the first century.

Now remember the temptation the Galatians were facing—they were being enticed to accept circumcision, along with the rest of the Mosaic requirements. This would involve the ancient Israelite calendar, with all its anticipation of Christ, as though He had not come. Such cyclic observance of times (as a spiritual duty) is infantilism. Does this same temptation occur for those who follow the Christian calendar year? Yes, it most certainly can, depending on why the seasons are observed, and how they are observed. It can also happen to those who refuse to define their year in terms of Christ, and find themselves observing Labor Day and Memorial Day instead.

Paul is assuming that God has really intervened in the lives of the Galatians. He assumes that they are known of God. At the same time, he fears that his labor with them may have been in vain. Nothing is more apparent than the fact that Paul is dealing with the Galatians in covenantal terms. He is not saying that he, Paul, has seen the secret decree concerning them. But he does know their place in the covenant. Because he has not seen the decree, he fears that they might fall. They are showing clear signs of their readiness to fall. But because he knows their standing in Christ, he speaks of them as known by God in the covenant. He does not treat apostasy and perseverance as an abstract math problem. He interacts with them as visible saints, and calls them to make their calling and election sure.

CHRIST FORMED IN YOU

The outline of Paul's appeal is now plain. He then turns to make a personal appeal to the Galatians. Their potential apostasy involves much more than simply following an argument—although it includes that. That "much more" has to do with their personal relationship with Paul himself.

> Brethren, I beseech you, be as I am; for I am as ye are: ye have not injured me at all. Ye know how through infirmity of the flesh I preached the gospel unto you

at the first. And my temptation which was in my flesh
ye despised not, nor rejected; but received me as an
angel of God, even as Christ Jesus. Where is then the
blessedness ye spake of? for I bear you record, that, if
it had been possible, ye would have plucked out your
own eyes, and have given them to me. Am I therefore
become your enemy, because I tell you the truth? They
zealously affect you, but not well; yea, they would
exclude you, that ye might affect them. But it is good
to be zealously affected always in a good thing, and not
only when I am present with you. My little children, of
whom I travail in birth again until Christ be formed in
you, I desire to be present with you now, and to change
my voice; for I stand in doubt of you. (Gal. 4:12–20)

Paul begins with an appeal to switch places and says that
they did not injure him (v. 12). The reason he preached to
them in the first place involved an infirmity (v. 13). Paul
could have been despised for that reason then, but the Galatians received him as an angel, or even as Jesus Himself (v.
14). At that time, his presence with them was blessed and
they had said so (v. 15). They would have taken out their
own eyes to give them to Paul, which indicates that his infirmity probably had something to do with his eyes. What did
Paul do to become their enemy? Was it telling the truth (v.
16)? The Judaizers were zealously courting the Galatians,
but in order to *exclude* them. That would in turn have caused
the Galatians to become the "suitors" (v. 17). Zeal is good,
but not when it is haphazard (v. 18). In a gloriously tangled
metaphor, Paul is in labor until Christ is formed in them,

meaning Christ is being formed in him through their sancti-
fication (v. 19). Paul is baffled and wants to be with them so
he can look at their faces while he talks (v. 20).

Paul felt the same way about the Galatians away from
them as he had felt when he was with them (vv. 18–19).
But they did not return the favor. He was an angel of God
when he was present (v. 14), but one to be rejected when
absent (v. 16). They *forgot* their previous blessing of Paul.
An inconstant man is greatly affected by his surroundings. A
constant man understands the nature of loyalty, and his circumstances do not blow his loyalties about. An inconstant
man is like a thermometer, reflecting the temperature of
the surrounding room. A constant man is like a thermostat,
affecting the temperature of the surrounding room.

We also see in Paul the psychology of true Christian leadership. Jesus warned His disciples not to imitate the leadership techniques of the Gentiles. He put it this way:

> But Jesus called them to Himself and said, "You know
> that the rulers of the Gentiles lord it over them, and
> those who are great exercise authority over them.
> Yet it shall not be so among you; but whoever desires
> to become great among you, let him be your servant.
> And whoever desires to be first among you, let him be
> your slave—just as the Son of Man did not come to be
> served, but to serve, and to give His life a ransom for
> many." (Matt. 20:25–28)

Some Christian leaders disobey Christ's instruction
because they are glory-hounds. But it must be noted that

others disobey it because they are shrewd pragmatists. Mistreatment of people "works." Paul makes this plain elsewhere. "For you put up with it if one brings you into bondage, if one devours you, if one takes from you, if one exalts himself, if one strikes you on the face. To our shame, I say that we were too weak for that! But in whatever anyone is bold—I speak foolishly—I am bold also" (2 Cor. 11:20–21). He points to the same reality here. The Galatians are listening to the Judaizers because they are *excluding* them so that they could then try to earn their inclusion (v. 17). Paul had simply preached the good news of their *accomplished* inclusion—where is the challenge in that? So they became his enemy because he presented the *truth* of the gospel to them, the truth of *good news* to them. This is why faithful shepherds are frequently accused of tyranny, and why tyrants are not. Tyrants have no lack of sycophants who will praise their kindness. And faithful Christians like Paul have no lack of accusers who are not afraid to lie.

Now what is before us as Christians today? It is the same process that the Galatians were going through. Christ is being formed in you, and this results in turmoil for both you and your pastors. God did not intend for this process to be simple. But He did intend for the end result to be glorious—which is Christ *fully formed* in you.

ALL SPIRITUAL WISDOM

The meaning of the two sons in this passage is absolutely basic to all spiritual wisdom. If we listen to carnal whispers we will get this all tangled up—and we must not.

Tell me, ye that desire to be under the law, do ye not hear the law? For it is written, that Abraham had two sons, the one by a bondmaid, the other by a freewoman. But he who was of the bondwoman was born after the flesh; but he of the freewoman was by promise. Which things are an allegory: for these are the two covenants; the one from the mount Sinai, which gendereth to bondage, which is Agar. For this Agar is mount Sinai in Arabia, and answereth to Jerusalem which now is, and is in bondage with her children. But Jerusalem which is above is free, which is the mother of us all. For it is written, Rejoice, thou barren that bearest not; break forth and cry, thou that travailest not: for the desolate hath many more children than she which hath an husband. Now we, brethren, as Isaac was, are the children of promise. But as then he that was born after the flesh persecuted him that was born after the Spirit, even so it is now. Nevertheless what saith the scripture? Cast out the bondwoman and her son: for the son of the bondwoman shall not be heir with the son of the freewoman. So then, brethren, we are not children of the bondwoman, but of the free. (Gal. 4:21–31)

Those Galatians who desire to be under the law have this problem—they are refusing to listen to the law (v. 21). Abraham had two sons. Ishmael was born of the concubine Hagar, and Isaac was born of the free wife, Sarah (v. 22). The son of the slave woman was after the flesh, but the son of Sarah was the fulfillment of promise (v. 23). Now, Paul says, messing with our modernity, this is an allegory. Sinai corresponds to Hagar, which corresponds to Jerusalem below, all of which tend to spiritual bondage over generations (vv. 24–25). But the heavenly Jerusalem is free and is our spiritual mother (v. 26). Paul quotes Isaiah 54 here. The barren woman is now more fruitful than the other woman (v. 27). We Christians, Paul says, are like Isaac—children of promise (v. 28). The analogy is wide-reaching. There is antipathy between the two children (v. 29). The children of the flesh are to be disinherited; they cannot be joint heirs (v. 30). Christians are the children of Sarah, not Hagar (v. 31).

Allegory causes us problems. In the late seventies, I took a summer course in hermeneutics from a well-known evangelical seminary. Our project was the book of Galatians, and when we got to this portion of the text, the instructor said that Paul was *wrong* to do what he did here. Allegorical interpretation was forbidden. While many would see this as extreme (and heretical), we still tend to share this gentleman's suspicions. If we interpret the Bible "allegorically," where are the brakes? What is to prevent us from careening off into a very baroque school of interpretation? There are two responses here. One is that we assume that our current mode of "interpreting" doesn't need brakes. And second, we have forgotten how much Scripture teaches us about types and allegories.

We need biblical eyes. The issue is not this particular passage or that one. The issue is not whether our handling of a passage could be tighter or not. The issue is how we think, how we respond. Do we let Scripture define everything in our lives, or do we try to have our lives (and our understanding) shape the Scriptures?

The Church is our mother. Sarah was a type of the Christian church. Her long years of barrenness correspond to her time in the old covenant. She was the wife of Abraham, but she was barren. Paul argues that the Jerusalem above is a woman who *used* to be barren, and who now has a multitude of children. She is the free woman—but there was a time when the free woman appeared to be fruitless and the slave woman appeared to be fruitful. The Church above is our mother. The heavenly Jerusalem is not built on a mountain that can be touched by human hands (Heb. 12:18ff). Come, the angel said, I will show you the bride, the wife of the Lamb. And John was shown the new Jerusalem, descending from heaven (Rev. 21:9–10). This is the Church, this is our mother.

And as we learn to relate to our mother, we will always be dealing with two kinds of children. There will always be Isaacs, and there will always be Ishmaels. This transition from the old covenant to the new is the point where Sarah has borne her freeborn son, and the slave woman is divorced and put away. Now are there no more temptations or pitfalls? Of course not. Until the world ends, there will always be those who live carnally in unbelief and those who live in faith, by faith, and unto faith. Over time, the ratios between these two groups change, but we are always dealing with them. But not only so, we will always be dealing with them *within the visible Church*. The new covenant is *not* the time when it becomes impossible to be an Ishmael.

We are promised that the children of the free woman will overrun the earth. Abraham was promised the world (Rom. 4:13), and his (free) children *will* possess it. And five years before the Last Trumpet, there will be some poor fool still clutching at his unbelief. This text summons us and commands us to be *unlike that man.* The just shall live by faith, and the meek will inherit the earth.

GALATIANS 5

TWO WAYS OF JUSTIFICATION

The lines of descent from Sarah and Hagar are *fluid*. In other words, physical sons of Sarah can become Ishmaelites through unbelief. Physical sons of Hagar can come in faith to Christ and be adopted into Israel. That which God uses to determine which way it goes is *faith*, which He imparts as a sovereign gift—faith now, faith alone, and faith forever. For this orthodox emphasis, some of us who hold firmly to this truth have been accused by some theologians—whose subtlety is wondrous to behold—of denying *sola fide*. How much there is to this foolishness we will see soon enough.

> Stand fast therefore in the liberty wherewith Christ hath made us free, and be not entangled again with the

yoke of bondage. Behold, I Paul say unto you, that if ye
be circumcised, Christ shall profit you nothing. For I testify again to every man that is circumcised, that he is a
debtor to do the whole law. Christ is become of no effect
unto you, whosoever of you are justified by the law; ye
are fallen from grace. For we through the Spirit wait for
the hope of righteousness by faith. For in Jesus Christ
neither circumcision availeth any thing, nor uncircumcision; but faith which worketh by love. Ye did run well;
who did hinder you that ye should not obey the truth?
This persuasion cometh not of him that calleth you. A
little leaven leaveneth the whole lump. (Gal. 5:1–9)

We have just finished learning that sons of unbelief are
sons of Hagar. Sons of faith are sons of Sarah—they are
children of the promise. But to start with promise and try
to finish with human effort (Gal. 3:1) is to fall into apostasy.
This is how sons of Sarah over time became sons of Hagar.
Now, Paul says, you Galatians must stand fast in your liberty (v. 1). Paul has just finished saying that the Galatians
are children of the free woman (4:31). But now, in the next
breath, he says that if they accept circumcision, Christ will
profit them nothing (v. 2). Back to Hagar. Why is this? If a
man accepts circumcision (in this context), he is obligated to
keep the entire law on his own steam (v. 3). Christ is ineffec-
tual for him. Those who seek justification through the law
have fallen from grace (v. 4). But we (through the Spirit)
wait for the hope of justification by faith (v. 5). In Jesus, it
is neither circumcision nor uncircumcision, but rather faith
working in love (v. 6). The Galatians had started their race

well—who was it that got in their way so that they did not obey the truth (v. 7)? This opinion they were entertaining was not from the Holy Spirit (v. 8). A little works leavens a big lump of grace (v. 9).

What is the lens of the covenant? Paul is confronted with a pastoral problem in the churches of Galatia. He is not confronted with a logical problem in systematics class in a seminary. People who fall away from the Church are falling away from grace. They are falling away from Christ. We are not saying that they have fallen away from the eternal secret decree of election. Of course not. If we ask if someone can fall away from the secret decree of election, the answer is obviously *no*. But that is the logic problem. If all dogs have four legs, and this is a dog, then this has four legs. If all the secret elect are predestined to glory, and this person is among the secret elect, then this person is predestined to glory. Great, and amen. But we do not have possession of the contents of the secret decree (Deut. 29:29). We are to walk by faith and not by sight. We do see the covenant, and the presence of Christ in it. That is, we see Christ in the covenant with the eyes of *faith*. But if we start adding other ways to justify ourselves before God, then we have fallen from grace because of our manifest unbelief.

The issue is not this particular passage or that one. The issue is not whether our handling of a passage could be tighter or not. The issue is how we think, how we respond. Do we let Scripture define everything in our lives, or do we try to have our lives (and our understanding) shape the Scriptures?

There are only two means of justification, *and one of them doesn't work*. One is self-justification, and the other is

Christ-justification. If anyone is circumcised (with this idol
of self-justification in his heart), then he is bound over to
self-perfection, which is impossible. But the problem is the
idol, not the circumcision. The same thing goes for baptism,
lack of baptism, Westminster-confessing, lack of it, memorizing the catechism, hating catechisms, and so on. This is
not complicated. At the end of all the rationalizations, it is
this question: self or Christ?

Those who are true sons of Sarah are those who through
the Spirit wait for a future hope—a future justification, a
future righteousness (v. 5). How do we wait for this? We
wait for it by faith, in faith, through faith. There is a sense in
which the elect are already justified at their conversion, but
there is this sense here also. We look *forward* to it, and we
do so by faith. But note that here Paul is speaking of justification as some sort of future event. The word has more than
one scriptural meaning.

It is hard to run, and easy to trip someone who is run-
ning. It is easy to persuade contrary to the teaching of the
Spirit. Leaven works through the whole lump silently, easily,
and readily. It does not need to be coaxed. And the leaven
of works does corrupt grace. The human heart takes naturally to self-flattery and loves any religion that will help this
process of flattery along. The problem with the critics of the
"objective covenant" is therefore not that they are too critical
and cautious. The problem is that they are not nearly cautious enough. We are justified by faith, through faith in Jesus.
We are not justified through faith in justification by faith.

In this world, Christians can be Christians in two senses.
One sense is when they are part of the visible Church, when

they are baptized, and this is shared by elect and non-elect alike. The other sense is when a person is effectually called by the Spirit of God, baptized by Him into the number of the regenerate. This latter sense is the *only* sense that is salvific. Just as an unfaithful man can be objectively a husband, so an unregenerate man can be objectively a Christian—meaning that he can be part of the visible Church.

LOVE AND POLEMICS

We have already seen that the lines of descent from Sarah and Hagar are *fluid*. We are now coming to the great truth that the family resemblance borne in these lines is also *obvious*. Sons of Abraham do the works of Abraham. This passage closes on the threshold of Paul's great description of the two lines of the children of men, and how he builds up to this is very important.

> I have confidence in you through the Lord, that ye will be none otherwise minded: but he that troubleth you shall bear his judgment, whosoever he be. And I, brethren, if I yet preach circumcision, why do I yet suffer persecution? then is the offence of the cross ceased. I would they were even cut off which trouble you. For, brethren, ye have been called unto liberty; only use not liberty for an occasion to the flesh, but by love serve one another. For all the law is fulfilled in one word, even in this; Thou shalt love thy neighbour as thyself. But if ye bite and devour one another, take heed that ye be not consumed one of another. This I say then, Walk in

the Spirit, and ye shall not fulfil the lust of the flesh.
For the flesh lusteth against the Spirit, and the Spirit
against the flesh: and these are contrary the one to the
other: so that ye cannot do the things that ye would.
But if ye be led of the Spirit, ye are not under the law.
(Gal. 5:10–18)

Paul expresses his confidence that the Galatians will
not in fact fall away (v. 10). But this is his faith in the final
outcome; Paul is not complacent about it—if he had been,
there was no need for this letter. But the troublemaker will
bear his own judgment. Paul points out that if he was still
preaching circumcision, he would not be in the trouble he
was in. Circumcision removes the offense of the cross (v.
11). Paul then wishes that those zealous for circumcision
would overachieve (v. 12). He desires this because the Galatians were called to liberty and love (v. 13). The entire law
is summed up in the second greatest commandment (v. 14).
In contrast to this, biting and devouring one another would
destroy them all (v. 15). Walking in the Spirit and fulfilling
the lusts of the flesh are mutually inconsistent (v. 16). In
fact, the two are at war with one another (v. 17). And if you
are under the Spirit, you are not under the law (v. 18).

When it comes to justification, faith and works do not
go together. Paul is confident that the Galatians will hear
him (v. 10). He is also certain that the one who got them
all stirred up will bear his judgment. This is not a mere
academic debate. Paul fights this as an evangelist, and
not as a detached, academic scholar. But even though
Paul is confident that the Galatians will not fall away, he

has nevertheless been distressed by their actions, and has rebuked them strongly for those actions. It is like Paul and the impending shipwreck (Acts 27:22, 31). He knows the outcome, but we still have personal responsibility. Calvinism is not fatalism.

Immediately after his expression of confidence, Paul points out that if he were still preaching circumcision (as a requirement for Gentiles), then he would not be assaulted as he was being assaulted. To admit the requirement of circumcision was to remove the offense of the cross (v. 11). Religious self-sufficiency is (in every age) insulted by the cross. And those who preach the cross will always find themselves in trouble. Now a simple question: would the Judaizers in Galatia accept *this* description of their teaching? No, but that is not the point. The description was still true.

Paul then delivers a remarkable polemical blow. He wishes that the Judaizers (the troublers) were "cut off." This layered insult is about as offensive as it was possible to be. The word (*apokopto*) means to castrate, which would exclude an old covenant worshipper from the Temple (Deut. 23:1). It would also identify the religion of the Judaizers with pagan castration, which was common. It also caricatures what they were demanding of the Galatians, which was circumcision. So this was the mother of all insults.

But in the next breath . . . without missing a beat, Paul then tells the Galatians to love one another. They were called to liberty, but they were not to use their liberty to indulge the flesh (v. 13). Remember that flesh here does *not* mean physical body. The flesh in this sense for Paul is the principle of rebellion, and is part of our remaining sinfulness.

They were called to insult the flesh, not indulge it. That is what Paul has just finished doing—he insulted the religious flesh-mongers. And that is what he wants the Galatians to do as well. This is not merely consistent with love; it is the foundation of it. The law is fulfilled in love, not in circumcision (v. 14). For love and circumcision to make a peace treaty is for the flesh to defeat the Spirit. So Paul says not to bite and devour one another—which the religion of the Judaizers will necessarily lead to (v. 15).

There are only two ways to walk. Either we will walk in the Spirit or we will walk in the flesh (v. 16). We will see the descriptive characteristics of each in the next section. Here we see that it is one way or the other. The two cannot be combined into a third way because the two ways are mortal enemies (v. 17). They contend against one another, and the one excludes the other (v. 18). In a fallen world, love is not indiscriminate or promiscuous. If a doctor loves cancer, then he hates cancer patients. If a shepherd loves wolves, he hates sheep. If a farmer loves the weeds, he hates the crop. And if we love the flesh, as Paul describes it here, then we hate the Spirit. Not only so, but we hate His work, His fruit, His children, and His promises.

Now what does love look like? What does hate look like? What does polemical discourse, over the souls of men, look like? The Scriptures *do not leave this question unanswered.*

REALLY OBVIOUS

The principle is firmly established already. Paul is building up to the point that false religion is the foundation of all false living. Just as believing lives are built upon the truth of God, so false lives are built on the lies of righteousness-mongers.

> But if ye be led of the Spirit, ye are not under the law. Now the works of the flesh are manifest, which are these; Adultery, fornication, uncleanness, lasciviousness, Idolatry, witchcraft, hatred, variance, emulations, wrath, strife, seditions, heresies, Envyings, murders, drunkenness, revellings, and such like: of the which I tell you before, as I have also told you in time past, that they which do such things shall not inherit the kingdom of God. But the fruit of the Spirit is love, joy, peace, longsuffering, gentleness, goodness, faith, Meekness, temperance: against such there is no law. And they that are Christ's have crucified the flesh with the affections and lusts. If we live in the Spirit, let us also walk in the Spirit. Let us not be desirous of vain glory, provoking one another, envying one another. (Gal. 5:18–26)

Those who are led by the Spirit are not under the law, which is where the Judaizers are in effect trying to get them (v. 18). But the Judaizers want them to go to the religious rite of circumcision, and not into a frenzy of wicked behavior. But Paul says this is where they will in fact wind up, because religiosity does not deal with the flesh but rather caters to it. The works of the flesh, Paul says, are *obvious* (v. 19). He then gives a detailed catalog of such offenses (vv. 19–21). In contrast, the way of the Spirit is equally obvious (vv. 22–23). Those who belong to Christ have crucified the flesh, along with everything it wants (v. 24). But remember that at the head of the list of things the flesh wants, we must include religious respectability. If we are alive in the Spirit, then why not walk as though this were so (v. 25)? And Paul returns to the engine that is driving all this—*vain glory*—and he urges them to avoid provocation and envy (v. 26).

It is not just that the content of these two lists is different. They are qualitatively two lists of different *kinds* of things. The *wages* of sin is death, but the *gift* of God is eternal life (Rom. 6:23). Here the same point is made with the contrast between the *works* of the flesh and the *fruit* of the Spirit. Heaven is a gift, and Hell is a paycheck.

The problem with various forms of pietism is *not* that it is believed that the internal condition of a man will necessarily be evident in his life, but rather that pietism refuses to identify the external symptoms of the internal condition biblically. We make the indicator simplistic like "drinking beer" or "coming to prayer meeting." We need to look at the characteristics that God gives. They are *obvious*, Paul says.

These works are manifest. Out of the abundance of the heart a man speaks (Matt. 12:34). Out of the abundance of the heart a man lives (Matt. 12:35).

> Adultery: a narrow term, meaning violation of an existing marriage covenant.

> Fornication: a broad term, meaning sexual uncleanness generally. This would of course include pornography.

> Uncleanness: dirty living, whether physical or spiritual.

> Lasciviousness: wantonness, unbridled lust.

Idolatry: worship of false gods, including the god of money.

Witchcraft: magical arts, as well as the use of drugs.

Hatred: enmity, hatred, bitterness, malice.

Variance: wrangling, jangling, strife, and quarreling.

Emulations: envying, indignation, jealousy.

Wrath: anger, passion, heat.

Strife: partisanship, politicking, fractiousness.

Seditions: division, schism.

Heresies: sectarianism, schism, gathering around an error, leprosy of the mind.

Envyings: envying, biting.

Murders: slaughter, murder, hatred.

Drunkenness: to be intoxicated.

Revellings: carousal, reveling late at night, raucous parties.

And such like: the list is *not* intended to be exhaustive, but rather representative.

The fruit of the Spirit stands in stark contrast to all such works of the flesh.

Love: glad and sacrificial giving of one's self.

Joy: gladness and deep confidence in the goodness of God.

Peace: calmness, contentment, tranquility, serenity.

Longsuffering: patience, endurance, constancy, stead-
fastness, perseverance, forbearance, and slowness in
avenging wrongs.

Gentleness: goodness, kindness, integrity.

Goodness: uprightness of heart and life.

Faith: assurance, belief, fidelity.

Meekness: gentleness, mildness.

Temperance: self-control, balance.

Those who are baptized have been baptized into Christ,
which means they have been baptized "into" the second
list. But what if their life still matches the first list? What
does that mean? It means that, apart from repentance, they
will not inherit the kingdom of God. Their baptism obli-
gates them covenantally to be characterized by the second
list, not the first. But unbelief within the covenant makes
disobedience within the covenant possible. Baptism puts a
man under the obligations of the covenant; it does not sub-
stitute for a life of obedience *based on faith in Christ alone.*
And this is why the false doctrine of the Judaizers must be
rejected. Their approach to religion caters to the flesh, and
cannot mortify the deeds of the flesh, even if it wanted to,
which it actually does not. Religiosity kills. Traditional val-
ues inflame the lusts of the heart. Common decency is a
whitewashed tomb.

GALATIANS 6

SOWING AND REAPING

Paul has already told us that the works of the flesh and the fruit of the Spirit are inconsistent with one another. But a problem is caused because people who live in accordance with the two "lists" have to associate with one another, both in the world and in the Church. *Now* what? There is a certain amount of jumbling for the time being.

> Brethren, if a man be overtaken in a fault, ye which are spiritual, restore such an one in the spirit of meekness; considering thyself, lest thou also be tempted. Bear ye one another's burdens, and so fulfil the law of Christ. For if a man think himself to be something, when he is nothing, he deceiveth himself. But let every man

77

prove his own work, and then shall he have rejoicing
in himself alone, and not in another. For every man
shall bear his own burden. Let him that is taught in the
word communicate unto him that teacheth in all good
things. Be not deceived; God is not mocked: for what-
soever a man soweth, that shall he also reap. For he that
soweth to his flesh shall of the flesh reap corruption;
but he that soweth to the Spirit shall of the Spirit reap
life everlasting. And let us not be weary in well doing:
for in due season we shall reap, if we faint not. As we
have therefore opportunity, let us do good unto all men,
especially unto them who are of the household of faith.
(Gal. 6:1–10)

What is the alternative to biting and devouring (the
besetting sin of the religiously scrupulous)? It is obviously the life of the Spirit, and Paul talks here about how
a Spirit-led man functions in this very messy world. If
someone else stumbles, a man must be qualified to correct
him before he undertakes that task (v. 1). We are called to
share the load, one with another (v. 2). But there are those
who do not grasp the situation rightly, or their own role in
it (v. 3). Objective testing is most necessary (v. 4). Carry-
ing one another's burdens is not a replacement for pulling
your own weight (v. 5). Those who are taught should seek
out ways to bless the teacher (v. 6). This is the context for
the famous phrase that a man reaps what he sows (v. 7).
There are only two possible crops—flesh and Spirit (v. 8).
Agriculture is not an "instant" kind of business (v. 9). We
therefore are to "sow" good in the field of all men, but we

should pay special attention to one portion of the field—
the household of faith (v. 10).

How should we bear one another's burdens? It is not the
case that everyone in the Church is equally wise. It is not
the case that everyone does an equally good job staying
out of sin. And so this means that one person must frequently be put right by another. If someone sins, then one
who is spiritual should correct him, considering himself,
lest he also be tempted (v. 1). But too often when we are
motivated to correct, we are not qualified to do so, and
when we are qualified to do so, we are not motivated. This
means that our motivation has to change from personal
irritation to simple obedience.

Rather than seeing these comments as disjointed, ran-
dom observations, we should consider them as part of the
same context. Restoring someone after they have sinned
is part of bearing one another's burdens (v. 2). When do
you carry someone else's pack? When they have *fallen*. But
some men do not think they have fallen (v. 3). And some
men are not spiritually qualified to correct others like they
think they are (v. 3). So what do we do? Each man is to test
the quality of his work objectively, that is, with some reference beyond his own personal opinions (2 Cor. 10:12).
Then he can rejoice in what he has done (v. 4). This why
only the humble can have true job satisfaction.

Let us return for a moment to a point made above. Those
who feel like correcting others are not qualified to do so.
Those who are qualified to do so do not feel like it. And
herein lies a problem, especially in the management of the
household. Far too many parents correct their children when

they are not spiritually qualified to say or do *anything*. And when they *are* qualified to do their parental duty, they do not do it, remaining lazy and complacent. Why are the children disciplined? Are they disciplined because they need to be loved in this way? Or are they disciplined because Mom or Dad has a headache and "will not put up with that racket another *minute!*"

The one who is taught should *fellowship* in all good things with the one who teaches. The word for *communicate* is the verb form of *koinonia*, and this refers to everything from verbal thanks and gratitude to financial support, and many things between. "Do not be deceived," Paul says (and this is certainly a place where one *might* be). God is not mocked. How you treat those who teach and pastor you is the seed you are putting in the ground. But remember, this is broadly construed (*all* good things), not narrowly construed. In other words, a full and harmonious relationship between godly teachers and the taught is necessary to keep the ungodly teachers from getting into the field and planting a crop of Religious Flesh. And this harmonious relationship needs to be cultivated across the board.

And it is hard work to maintain. It is possible to get weary in that work, especially when false teachers are trying to undermine the entire process. And it is important to remember that harvest does not occur immediately after the obedience of plowing and planting. We are called to wait in hope. We will reap in due season, provided we do not get discouraged during the wait. This is why Christians need to be dedicated to doing good for all men. But since we are finite, we are not capable of doing the Universal Good Deed. We have to start somewhere. Paul tells us to start within the Church, and a key place to focus attention within the Church is on the relationship between teachers and taught. And when you start in the Church, you should make sure to start with the person right next to you. And *that* will be rewarded with a glorious harvest.

THE CRUCIFORM HEART

As we seek to gather in our hearts and minds the message of this wonderful book, we can see the heart of it here in the last passage. Just as we need to summarize, so does Paul.

> Ye see how large a letter I have written unto you with mine own hand. As many as desire to make a fair shew in the flesh, they constrain you to be circumcised; only lest they should suffer persecution for the cross of Christ. For neither they themselves who are circumcised keep the law; but desire to have you circumcised, that they may glory in your flesh. But God forbid that I should glory, save in the cross of our Lord Jesus Christ, by whom the world is crucified unto me, and I unto the world. For in Christ Jesus neither circumcision availeth any thing, nor uncircumcision, but a new creature. And as many as walk according to this rule, peace be on them, and mercy, and upon the Israel of God. From henceforth let no man trouble me: for I bear in my body the marks of the Lord Jesus. Brethren, the grace of our Lord Jesus Christ be with your spirit. Amen. (Gal. 6:11–18)

Paul's adversaries had lied about so many things it was quite possible that they would deny Paul even wrote this letter. So, Paul says, look at my handwriting (v. 11). Those who want to parade around in the flesh insist on circumcision for others. To do otherwise would threaten their comfort, incurring persecution for the cross. Can't have *that* (v. 12). They do what they do in the name of the law, but they do not keep it themselves. Their interest is the flesh, not the law of love (v. 13). But Paul glories in the cross alone, in which the world and the believer *die to one another* (v. 14). The point is not circumcision (in *either* direction), but rather a new creation (v. 15). Those who get this, peace and mercy are their benediction. The same goes for the Israel of God (v. 16). Let every man leave Paul alone, a man who has paid all his dues (v. 17). May the grace of Jesus Christ rest upon the Galatians' spirits (v. 18).

If a man cares about something outside himself, it is possible to appeal to him through argument, or appeal to duty, or through the attraction of that which is lovely. But if a man cares only for *himself*, keeping himself warm and dry, then it is no use to appeal to him through anything that might threaten that position. Everything that is said, no matter what is said, is incorporated into an ingenious argument that shows that he does not have to alter anything at all. When Paul hadn't written, they advanced their heresy. When he did, they advanced their heresy. When he makes sure they know he was the one writing this letter, they no doubt will move on to something else.

There are two kinds of comfort. The flesh likes religion. It provides the industrious with a good way to get money, women, reputation, and fame, or even more money. In such a situation, to preach the cross is the height of folly. Consequently, the history of the Church is filled with ecclesiastics whose eye was always on the main chance, shepherds who would feed only themselves. This is one sort of comfort.

Godly comfort is from the God of all comfort, who comforts us in our afflictions so that we might learn to comfort others in the same way (2 Cor. 1:1ff). In order to qualify for this comfort, a man must have been nailed to the cross of Christ (with regard to the world), and the world must have been nailed to the cross of Christ (with regard to that man). The cross of Christ reveals to us the mind of Christ, and it is in this cross that we finally learn to see the fundamental vanity of all worldly things. Note that I did not say all *earthly* things, or *material* things. But the world is described for us repeatedly in the New Testament. It is Vanity Fair, and those who start quibbling about whether this or that aspect of the fair is lawful in itself are simply showing that they are fools. But not to themselves, of course. Of *course* this or that is lawful.

The issue is always the heart. The issue is never circumcision or uncircumcision. It is not baptism or unbaptism. It is never membership in this church or that one. The issue is *why*. If the why is the new creation in the cross of Jesus Christ, everything else will be put to rights, and everything else will be a means of grace appropriated through faith alone. But in everything you say or do, provided it is in the name of God, someone will be right there to twist the words into something more conducive to the worldly way they want to remain.

Paul says that peace and mercy are for those who walk in accordance with this rule. Such an understanding is what ought to characterize the Israel of God, which is the Church. So what is the rule?

The rule is the cross. But not the cross on a steeple, or a little silver chain. The rule is not the cross in the architectural pattern of the church sanctuary. Of course, we are not opposed to the cruciform in all its various physical manifestations, but what we are really after is the cruciform heart. The cruciform heart is naturally hostile to the world and recognizes that world in all its manifest shapes and appearances. Often that worldliness is "cruciform." Sometimes it is hostile to that form. The world is a protean shapeshifter.

Confused? This is why Paul attacks the law, when it is in the mouths of those who would commend themselves. This is why he glories in the law when it is in the mouth of the one who loves. This is why Jeremiah attacked the Temple, and why Solomon built it. This is why God commanded sacrifices and then told the people He actually wanted mercy instead. This is why ministers baptize the repentant and then laugh at the baptism of the unrepentant. This is why the Westminster Confession is one of the glories of Western civilization, which it is, as well as a set of blinkers for Calvinistic workhorses. This is why the saints of God have been called many different things—Catholics, Puritans, Methodists—and why they have frequently been persecuted by men bearing the name of yesterday's godliness.

The worldly Bible teacher, in love with the flesh, wants everything to *stay put*. Sons of Sarah must always remain sons of Sarah. To say that sons of Sarah can somehow become sons of Hagar is to talk nonsense to him. He wants everything static so that he has a foolproof method for knowing what side he is on. But that is not how spiritual battles go.

EPHESIANS

EPHESIANS 1

A ll of Scripture is of course inspired by God, and so all of it is true, entirely true. But some places in the Scriptures appear to contain more truth per square inch than other places. All Scripture is equally authoritative and equally true, but not all Scripture is equally dense.

Ephesians appears to me to be one of those places.

So given how dense with truth the book of Ephesians is, I have decided to spend our time here a little differently than we have with the commentary on Galatians. What I would like to do is work through the book in an overview, taking a chapter at a time, and then to work through it again, going verse by verse.

At the same time, even so, considering the book of Ephesians a chapter at a time is a little bit like taking pictures of
the Rocky Mountains from outer space. There is no hope of
covering everything; there is perhaps some hope of stirring
up a desire in you to give yourself to a lifetime of meditating
on the themes of this book, which perhaps might begin with
our second look at each chapter.

This epistle is traditionally divided into six chapters. In
each chapter, there is a first-pass flyover of the material, and
then the rest of the chapter walks through the same material. Because each chapter of the epistle has an overview,
and the rest of the chapter has a close verse-by-verse treatment, there will of necessity be some repetition. But as you
are a grown-up, you should just deal with it.

ONE OF THE CENTRAL JEWELS

As we learn later in this epistle, the Church is the bride of Christ.
As she is gloriously adorned for her husband on her wedding
day, she wears a golden crown, made up of all the Scriptures.
And if that image be allowed, the book of Ephesians should be
understood as one of the central jewels in that crown.

> Paul, an apostle of Jesus Christ by the will of God, to
> the saints which are at Ephesus, and to the faithful in
> Christ Jesus: Grace be to you, and peace, from God
> our Father, and from the Lord Jesus Christ. Blessed be
> the God and Father of our Lord Jesus Christ, who hath
> blessed us with all spiritual blessings in heavenly places
> in Christ . . . . (Eph. 1:1–23)

Ephesus was a harbor city on the west coast of modern Turkey. It was the capital city for Proconsular Asia and contained one of the seven wonders of the ancient world—the temple of Artemis (or Diana, to use the Latin name). It is a ruin today because the harbor silted up, and the remains of the city are well inland. But in Paul's day, a street called the Arcadian Way ran about half a mile east from the harbor, where it connected with the cross street called Theater Street. The theater itself—where the great riot occurred (Acts 19:29)—was straight across the street at the intersection. The city had a population of roughly 250,000. The city was a center of great learning, as well as of great superstitions (Acts 19:19). Paul lived there from A.D. 52–54, and this letter is written about ten years after that, from prison in Rome.

Paul begins by identifying himself as an apostle by the will of God, and he salutes the Ephesian saints as being faithful in Christ Jesus (v. 1). He blesses them with grace and peace from the Father and the Son (v 2). The Spirit is not mentioned by name because He *is* that grace and peace. A blessing is pronounced upon the Father of Jesus Christ, who is Himself the source of all spiritual blessings in the heavenly places in Christ (v. 3). The first mentioned blessing is the fact that we were chosen in Christ to be holy before the foundation of the world (v. 4). We were chosen to *be* holy, not because we *were* holy. He predestined us in love to be adopted by Jesus Christ and brought to God, and He did this because it was what He wanted to do (v. 5).

The result of this is so that the glory of His grace would be praised, not vilified (v. 6). We have redemption through

His blood, which means forgiveness for sin, according to His riches of grace (v. 7). This is a mountain of grace, but He did not just dump it on us; He showered us with this grace in all wisdom and prudence (v. 8). He lavishes, but with precision. God intended this within His own counsels for a long time past, from before the world was made, but has now unveiled the mystery to us (v. 9).

That mystery was that, when the time was finally right, God would gather everything in heaven and earth up into Christ (v. 10). In Christ, absolutely everything is recapitulated or summed up. God does everything just as He wishes, and His wishes included making us His heirs (v. 11). Paul is describing himself here as inundated by the first wave of this grace (v. 12). But Gentile Ephesians need not fear that this grace will run out—they also heard and believed and were sealed (v. 13). They were sealed by the Spirit, who is the earnest payment or first installment of their final inheritance (v. 14).

Ever since Paul heard of their faith in Jesus and love for the saints (v. 15), he had not stopped giving thanks for them (v. 16). His prayer for them included some remarkable requests—that the Father of glory would give them the spirit of wisdom and revelation in their knowledge of Christ (v. 17). He asks further that the eyes of their understanding would be enlightened to the extent that they would really "*get*" the hope of His calling, and the riches of the glory of *His* inheritance in the saints (v. 18)—a real down-is-up truth. How can wretched sinners make up *His* inheritance?

Another thing was the greatness of His power for believers (v. 19), the kind of power that was evidenced in the resurrection and ascension (v. 20). That ascension placed

Christ far above all current and future authorities (v. 21). Everything was placed under His feet (v. 22), and He was made head over everything for the Church. That Church is His body, the fullness of Him who fills everything (v. 23).

What is the real nature of Paul's prayer here? We are told that Jesus was exalted to the highest imaginable place—it says that He was raised *far above* every other authority in the cosmos (v. 21). But this is not why Paul asks for the eyes of their hearts to be enlightened. That is not the thing that staggers us; everyone expects God to be "far above" everything. Of course. He is God, after all.

The thing that would require a special anointing from the Spirit to "get" is the coupling of this exaltation of Christ with the honoring of His bride. Consider what Paul is actually saying here. First, before the foundation of the world, God chose *us* (v. 4), loved *us* (vv. 4–5), predestined *us* (v. 5), blessed *us* (v. 6), lavished grace upon *us* (v. 8), and so on. Second, Paul specifically says that he is asking that the Spirit would open their eyes so that they might understand how great and glorious Christ's inheritance is *in the saints* (v. 18). And third, we are told that Christ fills absolutely everything (v. 23), but in the same breath we are told that we in the Church are *His* fullness (v. 23). So the issue is not the exaltation of Christ; the issue is the corresponding exaltation of the Church in Christ.

If we get just a portion of what Paul is talking about here, we will buckle at the knees. If we are to learn this without collapsing, God will have to do it. Your condition before conversion and your condition now can only be compared to Christ in the tomb and Christ at the right hand of Almighty God.

So then there are two great themes in Ephesians—the reconciliation of all things in creation to Christ, and the reconciliation of all nations in Christ. All the practical teach-ing that is also contained here is simply learning how to live as if these two great themes are true.

VERSE BY VERSE

If the book of Ephesians were a great mansion, the first chap-ter would be the deep trenches where the concrete footings are poured. Every single thing that happens in the history of the world does so because it was determined beforehand by God. God works out everything "after the counsel of his own will," which means that this is the foundation for the superstructure of all human history. If that is the case, and it is, it also means that God's absolute foreordination sup-ports the rest of the book of Ephesians as well. As you work through the first chapter, your thought ought to be "God knows what He is doing, and He is doing it all."

> Paul, an apostle of Jesus Christ by the will of God, to the saints which are at Ephesus, and to the faithful in Christ Jesus (Eph. 1:1)

Paul's apostleship did not originate in the mind of Paul, but in the will of God the Father. As a result, Jesus Christ commissioned him to be an apostle and sent him out. We also see here that Jesus Christ acts in accordance with the will of His Father. What the Father determines, the Son enacts. The Father determined to send Paul, and so Jesus Christ did the sending.

The word *saints* is used here synonymously with believ-ers or Christians. Contrary to popular usage, the word *saint* here is not describing some kind of a super-Christian. Nevertheless, we *do* see that Paul calls the saints the "faithful in Christ Jesus." All the saints, all Christians, are described as the *faithful* in Christ. This is because a saint is someone who has been sanctified or "set apart." God sanctifies to a purpose, and that purpose includes faithfulness in Christ.

We see also that these saints are located in two places. They are *in Ephesus*, which tells us their position in the visible Church, the historical Church. This is the Church as recorded by countless church directories. These saints are also *in Christ*, a phrase that is used over thirty times in this epistle, which tells us they are being addressed as genuine Christians, as members of the invisible Church.

> Grace be to you, and peace, from God our Father, and
> from the Lord Jesus Christ. (Eph. 1:2)

Grace can be considered here as the continued unearned blessings God gives us in and through Christ. Peace is the ongoing result of the reconciliation which God accomplished for us in the cross. This salutation is close to what is said at the beginning of every epistle in the New Testament. Two gifts, grace and peace, are given to the saints from two persons, the Father and the Son. It is curious that the Holy Spirit is never mentioned in these initial greetings, and I would follow the suggestion of Jonathan Edwards that this is because the Spirit *is* the grace and peace. This in turn indicates that the grace and peace are not an impersonal spiritual juice, given to us so that we might have an extra spring in our step. God gives us grace by giving us Himself. In addition, we see how readily this fits with the *Filioque* of the Nicene Creed. The Holy Spirit is from both the Father and the Son.

> Blessed be the God and Father of our Lord Jesus Christ, who hath blessed us with all spiritual blessings in heavenly places in Christ. (Eph. 1:3)

God is blessed by Paul for all His blessings. This blessing is directed to the God and Father of the Lord Jesus. Why? Because of how He has blessed us. Where has He blessed us? In the heavenly realms. If someone were to ask what these heavenly realms are, or where they are, the answer is that the heavenly realms are where Christ is.

This has occurred for us because He has placed us *in Christ*. How has He blessed us? Every possible blessing has been given to us. This means that He has blessed us extensively. Paul is speaking in superlatives. Again, this is only because we are now *in Christ*.

> According as he hath chosen us in him before the foundation of the world, that we should be holy and without blame before him in love (Eph. 1:4)

In Scripture, discussion of election and predestination do not have the same tone of many of the treatments of the same subjects elsewhere. Scripture simply takes these things for granted and mentions them easily. The biblical writers show no embarrassment or shame over the fact that God is God, and we are not. He elects, and we do not. He chooses, and we therefore choose.

But neither do the biblical discussions of the subject confirm the many caricatures of predestination. This is because the Scripture concentrates on how *wonderful* these purposes of God are, and shows how consistent they are with His character. But men tend to treat the subject as though we have the right to sit in judgment on those purposes. But how can we judge what we cannot comprehend?

Here Paul is addressing predestination to godliness. God selected us to be *holy*. In this verse, we learn that God decided that Christians were to be holy and blameless. That decision came before the world's creation.

This can be said of all Christians even though Paul changes his use of pronouns in verse 13. He begins the book talking of "we" and then shifts to include Gentile believers (2:11; 3:1) halfway through the first chapter. Some might argue that only the apostles, or certain first century Jews, were therefore predestinated. This cannot be sustained in the light of the basic mystery that is presented in Ephesians. The point is to obliterate distinctions between Jew and Gentile, not to establish another kind of distinction. In verse 11 of the first chapter, the "we" obtained an inheritance, being predestinated to it. In verses 13–14, the Gentiles are included in *that same inheritance*.

> Having predestinated us unto the adoption of children
> by Jesus Christ to himself, according to the good plea-
> sure of his will (Eph. 1:5)

Here predestination is seen as an exhibition of God's love. It is not seen as a reason to accuse God of injustice. Those who do so do not understand that pots have no right to evaluate the potter's decisions and, on top of that, are in no position to evaluate the potter's character. He is *good*, and He is ultimately good.

This predestination is to our adoption as sons. In Romans 8:23, we learn that this adoption will occur at the redemption of our bodies. Later in Ephesians (4:30), Paul looks forward to the "day of redemption." When Jesus returns and we see Him as He is, then we will be changed. We will receive the resurrection body, which is our day of redemption. This event completes our adoption as sons.

There is a sense in which Christians can be called sons of God now (John 1:12; 1 John 3:1), but our adoption is not completed until the Lord Jesus comes and the dead are raised. It is this state of bodily redemption to which we are predestinated. This is accomplished by and through Jesus Christ. It is His will to do this; indeed, it is His pleasure. The decision to do this was according to His will, not ours.

So in this discussion of predestination, we find that this term is being applied to our final destination (resurrection) and not to our embarking for that destination (conversion).

This is not to say that God does not draw us to Himself at conversion, or that there is no electing decree that results in our conversion. It is simply to point out that the term *predestination* here appears to have a more specific application than we tend to give it. Instead of understanding election as a subset of predestination, we should understand it the other way around. We are predestined to be raised in glory, and this is a subset of His electing decree.

> To the praise of the glory of his grace, wherein he hath
> made us accepted in the beloved. (Eph. 1:6)

Having begun with praise, Paul now returns to praise. He has stated his reasons for praise, and we are now in a position to say *amen*. When the blessings we have been given in Christ are truly realized, we can do nothing but praise God's glorious grace. This grace of God is not given grudgingly; it is freely bestowed.

In order to be a recipient of this grace, I must be in Christ. The Father dearly loves the Son, so if we are in the One He loves, His grace is poured out on us. *God has never loved a sinner redemptively apart from Christ.* Notice also that the result of a proper understanding of predestination is praise. If that is not our response, then we do not have a biblical understanding of it.

> In whom we have redemption through his blood, the
> forgiveness of sins, according to the riches of his grace
> (Eph. 1:7)

Although we have not yet received the redemption of the body, we have been purchased from the slave market of sin. The ransom, or purchase price, is the blood of Jesus. We are therefore forgiven. This cleansing from sin can only occur *in Him*. In Him, His blood cleanses, and this is in accordance with the wealth of His grace.

Our redemption does not depend on the poverty of our feeble attempts at good works. It depends on the *riches* and *wealth* that the Scriptures call the grace of God. Salvation comes from God's storehouses, not ours.

> Wherein he hath abounded toward us in all wisdom
> and prudence (Eph. 1:8)

The storehouses mentioned above are not shut up. God lavishes His blessings on His elect. But He is not indiscriminate in His giving. He blesses, but with wisdom. He gives, but with understanding. God gives to our needs, and not necessarily to our wants. His grace is consistent with all wisdom and knowledge.

> Having made known unto us the mystery of his will,
> according to his good pleasure which he hath purposed
> in himself (Eph. 1:9)

The mystery of His will is a mystery no longer. It is something that has been revealed to His apostles, and through them to us. God has determined to accomplish something in Christ. This decision is based on His desire, His own good pleasure. What is this purpose? The answer to that question is the revelation of His mystery.

> That in the dispensation of the fulness of times he
> might gather together in one all things in Christ, both
> which are in heaven, and which are on earth; even in
> him (Eph. 1:10)

Before telling us what the revealed mystery is, Paul tells us when the unfolded mystery will occur. When the time is fulfilled, it will happen. History is not open-ended and directionless. It is moving toward a final culmination. The word under dispensation here is *oikonomian*, which could also be rendered as administration, or stewardship, or economy. It simply refers to how God chose to administer the fulfillment of all His promises throughout the Old Testament.

God's purpose in history is to bring all things in heaven and all things on earth together under the headship of Christ. Because we are in Him, this affects our destiny as well. We as believers are the instrument God uses to bring this about. As we pray, and preach the gospel, we bring every thought captive to Christ. Strongholds are torn down, and the headship of Christ is consequently acknowledged. In the fullness of time, it will be acknowledged everywhere—in heaven, on earth, and under the earth. Jesus Christ is Lord.

This acknowledgment occurs *in history*, prior to the culmination of all things.

> In whom also we have obtained an inheritance, being predestinated according to the purpose of him who worketh all things after the counsel of his own will: That we should be to the praise of his glory, who first trusted in Christ. (Eph. 1:11–12)

Again, God's choosing of us occurs *in Christ*. God's choice does not depend on our merit or will, but rather on His grace. Those of us who have been chosen have also been predestined to the praise of God's glory. This will happen on the day of redemption when we will see Christ as He is and become like Him. That happens on the day our bodies are resurrected. And under the control of God, *everything* works toward that day. When we are finally fully conformed to the image of Christ, God's glory will be revealed and praised. The inheritance of our salvation comes to us the same way salvation does. We have been saved, we are being saved, and we will be saved. We have received our inheritance, we are receiving our inheritance, and we will receive our inheritance. We have received the earnest payment already in the person of the Spirit (look ahead to v. 14), and so the final inheritance is guaranteed (2 Cor. 1:22; 5:5).

This is God's plan and it will be done. He is the one who works out *everything* in conformity to His will. Our predestination to Christlikeness is in accordance with God's plan for us. He will therefore accomplish it.

> In whom ye also trusted, after that ye heard the word of truth, the gospel of your salvation: in whom also after that ye believed, ye were sealed with that holy Spirit of promise (Eph. 1:13)

We were *chosen* in Christ before the creation of the world (v. 4). We were *included* in Christ at the moment of conversion. God predestinated us to holiness before the world began. He began the process in history when we were first included in Christ. That inclusion occurred when we first heard the Word of truth. This Word is the good news that brings salvation.

Up through verse 12, the apostle has been using the pronoun *we*. Here he turns and speaks to the Ephesians directly—"you also." It would be an error to suppose that the "we" were the recipients of God's predestinating redemptive love, and that the Ephesians were added later as a footnote or an afterthought. If Paul goes out of his way to include them in the grand themes he is discussing (for perhaps they were wondering if these blessings were for them as well), then we should not seek to exclude them and ourselves from God's predestinating redemptive love. The desire for such exclusion can only proceed from the all-too-common reluctance to embrace the biblical concept of the sovereignty of God.

In addition, such a distinction also has trouble with identifying the "we." The apostles? The first generation of Christians? Paul is teaching about *God*, who works out all things according to His will, and we cannot escape from His sovereign grace by disputing about pronouns.

> Which is the earnest of our inheritance until the redemption of the purchased possession, unto the praise of his glory. (Eph. 1:14)

Now that we are Christians, we have two assurances that we will indeed be finally and completely like Christ some day. God has given us His Word and He has given us His Spirit. God has given us a letter promising us a glorious inheritance in Christ. The promise is sealed in us and that seal is the Holy Spirit.

An earnest payment is a means of securing a purchase. When you put down an earnest payment on a house, it is a promise to pay the remainder. Here the Spirit is described as being that earnest payment. In order to secure our salvation, God gives *Himself* as the earnest payment. Because of this, our inheritance is guaranteed. God is so confident that

He will bring us safely to the day of redemption that He has given us the Holy Spirit as a deposit. A deposit is something kept by the recipient if the deal doesn't go through. If somehow we failed to receive the inheritance God promised, God forfeits His deposit—His Spirit. Because this is obviously impossible, no stronger guarantee can be given.

God has bought us with a price; we now belong to Him. He will bring His possession to that day of redemption. All the praise and all the glory go to Him.

> Wherefore I also, after I heard of your faith in the Lord Jesus, and love unto all the saints, cease not to give thanks for you, making mention of you in my prayers (Eph. 1:15–16)

Because all these things are true for those in Christ, Paul is truly thankful for the Ephesians. In his prayers for them, he thanks God that they have come to faith in the Lord Jesus and that they evidence a genuine love for all the saints. Given what Paul has said earlier, there are real reasons for thanksgiving. Notice here how faith in the Lord and love for His saints go together.

> That the God of our Lord Jesus Christ, the Father of glory, may give unto you the spirit of wisdom and revelation in the knowledge of him (Eph. 1:17)

Paul is not content to intercede for the saints at Ephesus in a vague, general way. In our intercession for other Christians, we should pattern our prayers after his. This is a great model for intercessory prayer. He prays that the Ephesians receive the Spirit of wisdom and revelation. The Father of our Lord Jesus is the Source of this gift. The result of receiving this gift is an increased knowledge of God. Paul's intercession on this point is continual; he *keeps* asking.

> The eyes of your understanding being enlightened; that ye may know what is the hope of his calling, and what the riches of the glory of his inheritance in the saints (Eph. 1:18)

Paul prays that the Ephesians begin to comprehend the hope to which God has called them. He wants them to know what God has in store for them. In order that they begin to grasp the knowledge of this hope, Paul prays that God give light to the eyes of their hearts. Having stated his desire, Paul goes on to discuss some of the aspects of this hope.

> The eyes of your understanding being enlightened; that ye may know what is the hope of his calling, and what the riches of the glory of his inheritance in the saints, and what is the exceeding greatness of his power to us-ward who believe, according to the working of his mighty power (Eph. 1:18–19)

This hope has two aspects. The first has to do with God's inheritance of us, His saints. There is a great day coming when *God* will inherit a glorious Church, without spot or any other blemish. And as God gives light to our hearts, we will begin to understand what He is doing; we will see what He is up to.

The second aspect has to do with the power which is at work within believers. This great power is incomparable—it cannot be compared to *anything*. Again, only God can give the understanding of this power.

> And what is the exceeding greatness of his power to us-ward who believe, according to the working of his mighty power, which he wrought in Christ, when he raised him from the dead, and set him at his own right hand in the heavenly places, far above all principality, and power, and might, and dominion, and every name that is named, not only in this world, but also in that which is to come (Eph. 1:19–21)

Although the power at work in us is incomparable, there is at least one display of power to which we can liken it. God showed His mighty strength when He raised Jesus from the dead and then raised Him up to the heavenly realms, where Jesus is now seated at the Father's right hand. The reason this incomparable power within us can be compared to the resurrection and ascension power is that it is really the same power—the power of God. God has worked mightily in Christ, just as He is working and will work mightily in us.

Because we are *in Christ*, we have been raised and we are also seated at the Father's right hand *in Christ*. It is important to remember that we are seated in Christ in the heavenly realms. When we come to discuss spiritual warfare (6:12), we will learn that this warfare is conducted in the heavenly realms as well. We are therefore to be strong *in the Lord* and in His mighty power.

Far above all principality, and power, and might, and
dominion, and every name that is named, not only in
this world, but also in that which is to come (Eph. 1:21)

God has exalted Jesus to a place that is second to none.
There is no position of authority in the universe which can
rival the authority of Jesus. Not only was this true in the age
in which Paul wrote, it is true in our age. Paul's age came to
a close with the destruction of Jerusalem in 70 A.D., and our
age, the age of the worldwide Christian conquest, began.
Human history used to be governed by the principalities
and powers, by fallen spiritual beings, but in the Christian
age, the Messiah is now the mediatorial Prince. The older
Judaic aeon gave way to the Christian aeon. We learn here
that the supremacy of Christ is the same now as it was in the
time of Paul. At the name of Jesus, every knee will one day
bow. And in Matthew 28:18, we learn that *all* authority has
been given to Christ.

And hath put all things under his feet, and gave him
to be the head over all things to the church, Which is
his body, the fulness of him that filleth all in all. (Eph.
1:22–23)

It is the Father who has placed Jesus in this position of
authority. He is the one who has appointed Jesus as head
over everything. Jesus exercises this headship on behalf of
the saints; it is for the Church. Jesus fills everything, and we
are His fullness. We are His fullness because we are His body,
His bride. Because we are in Christ and with Christ, we are

reigning with Him. The saints have been truly exalted by God in Christ. But only *in Christ*.

EPHESIANS 2

THE GLORY AND GRACE OF NEW BIRTH

The second chapter of Ephesians can be divided into three basic segments. The first describes the condition of man prior to regeneration (vv. 1–3). The second is a treatment of how God's grace works in such people, and the nature of the change accomplished in them (vv. 4–6). And the third is a description of the design God had in working such a transformation in them (vv. 7–22). All of it results—if we are paying attention—in a hymn of praise to the free grace and kindness of the most sovereign God.

> And you hath he quickened, who were dead in trespasses and sins; Wherein in time past ye walked

according to the course of this world, according to the
prince of the power of the air, the spirit that now worketh in the children of disobedience: Among whom also
we all had our conversation in times past in the lusts of
our flesh, fulfilling the desires of the flesh and of the
mind; and were by nature the children of wrath, even
as others . . . . (Eph. 2:1–22)

These Ephesian Gentiles were *dead* in their trespasses
and sins, and God made them alive again (v. 1). They had
been the *walking* dead, under the dominion of the prince
of evil, and in line with the world's corrupt way of doing
things (v. 2). Everybody has been in this condition ("we
all") and were therefore children of wrath by nature, walking in accordance with that nature (v. 3).

But God, motivated by the richness of His mercy and
the greatness of His love toward us (v. 4), quickened us
together with Christ (v. 5). This is the meaning of grace. He
has joined us in Christ to the resurrection of Jesus, and to
His ascension (v. 6).

The reason He did this was to put on a show for the
coming ages (v. 7)—a fireworks display of mercy, grace,
and kindness. The Ephesians were saved by grace through
faith, and not from themselves (v. 8). It is not by works—
contextually, *anything* autonomous, anything from ourselves (v. 9). For we are *God's* art project, fashioned for
good works (v. 10). We are saved *to* good works, not *by*
them. So the Ephesians should remember that they used to
be called Uncircumcision, Gentiles according to the flesh
(v. 11), and at that time they were utter outsiders (v. 12).

But now in Christ they are brought close to all those things they were so far away from before (v. 13). So the blood of Christ has now made them citizens of Israel, friends of the covenants of promise, full of hope, and possessors of God in the world.

Christ is therefore our peace, making one new man (Christian) out of the two men before (Jew and Gentile), and He did this by breaking down the middle wall of partition (v. 14). He did this by abolishing the laws of separation contained in the Mosaic law (v. 15), and in this He reconciled *both* unto God (v. 16). And so He preached peace to those who were far away from salvation, and those standing right next to it (v. 17). *Through* Jesus, everyone has access *by* one Spirit *to* the Father (v. 18). The Ephesian Gentiles are therefore no longer aliens but rather are fellow citizens with the saints, and full members of God's household (v. 19). Jesus is the cornerstone, the apostles and prophets are the foundation stones, and we are all being built upon that sure foundation (v. 20). With that foundation, the whole Temple (an organic and living Temple) grows, as we are being shaped and fashioned (v. 21). The whole point of this is to make a dwelling place for God (v. 22).

As we consider the teaching of this portion of the epistle, we need to reckon with three prepositions. In verse 18, we are given a glorious picture of the Trinitarian nature of prayer and the way we are now to approach God. First Paul says "we both," meaning Jews and Gentiles alike. Another way of saying this is "everybody." He then uses three prepositions to make his point—to, through, and by. We come *to* the Father, *through* the Son, *by* the Spirit. This is why, when we pray, we address the Father, and not Jesus. This is why, when we close our time of prayer, we pray in the name of Jesus, and not in the Father's name. And this is why the Spirit moves us to pray. Think of it this way—all three Persons are members of the Godhead, of course. But in the economy of salvation, the Father is the city we are driving to, the Son is the road, and the Spirit is the car.

When it comes to the living Temple, the apostle Peter uses a similar image, when he says that we are all living stones—stones for a Temple, and all the stones are *alive* (1 Pet. 2:4–5). Here Paul says that the Temple is being worked on ("fitly framed" and "builded together"), but he also says that the building *grows*. Given the quarry of death we were all brought from, it is striking that God uses us to build a Temple that is entirely alive. Dead stones are made—by regeneration—into living stones.

Our condition apart from the efficacious grace of God (by which I intend the new birth) is absolutely hopeless. Notice here the familiar triad of the "world, the flesh, and the devil." First, the world—he says the Ephesians walked "according to the course of this world" (v. 2). He says that they did this in accordance with their own nature ("by *nature* children of wrath" (v. 3). In this condition they pursued the desires of both flesh and mind. And then he says that this was under the prince of the power of the air, who exercises dominion over the children of disobedience (v. 2). There you have it—the world, the flesh, and the devil. Are you going to escape from this dungeon on your own? Not a chance.

Notice also that the covenants, ceremonies, circumcisions, incense, Scriptures, sacrifices, and membership in

Israel *did not fix this problem*. Saul had been "blameless" when it came to the law (Phil. 3:6), at least on paper, and yet here he includes himself in this mess that original sin created—we *all* were by nature children of wrath (v. 3).

This is how we can identify the glory and grace of the new birth. Dead means *dead*. And this means also that there is no salvation apart from a resurrection. If Christ is raised from the dead, and if that resurrection is imparted to you, then you are alive in Him. If not, then not. And you can be without this life even though you are a learned teacher in Israel, as Nicodemus was.

There is only death and life, and no third category in between them. Sprinkle water on a dead stone, and what you get is a wet stone, not a living one. Only *life* can impart life, and so baptism is only a blessing if it is done with living water. And it is only living water if it is Christ Himself. And Christ is only apprehended where there is true evangelical *faith* (vv. 8–9). Living faith—the gift of God, remember—transforms it all. It transforms dead faith, dead water, dead stones, dead people, dead religion, and any other dead thing we like (in our death) to carry around.

VERSE BY VERSE

The central lesson of chapter 2 is that man's spiritual predicament is one of being "dead and deep," meaning dead and long since buried. We were *dead* in our transgressions and sins. We were dead, not sick. And of course, this means that the unity that Jew and Gentile have in Christ was preceded by the unity that they had in the death grip of sin. All of us, Jews and Gentiles alike, were children of wrath by nature.

> And you hath he quickened, who were dead in tres-
> passes and sins (Eph. 2:1)

The result of all sin is death. Non-Christians are dead in their sins. Christians are dead to their sins. The difference is obvious. A non-Christian is dead to life. A Christian has died to death. It is equally obvious that a dead man can do nothing to effect his own resurrection. The state of death cannot be ended by those in it.

> Wherein in time past ye walked according to the course
> of this world, according to the prince of the power of
> the air, the spirit that now worketh in the children of
> disobedience (Eph. 2:2)

This condition of death is the unbeliever's natural habitat. His life is death. This death was caused by his bound disciple-ship to two things. Unbelievers follow the world and follow an evil spirit. The world has a certain way of operating. It works according to a certain pattern. Non-Christians simply follow the pattern, because "this is how things are done." They also follow an evil spirit, who is described as ruler of the kingdom of the air. This spirit is able to work in disobedient people.

> Among whom also we all had our conversation in times
> past in the lusts of our flesh, fulfilling the desires of the
> flesh and of the mind; and were by nature the children
> of wrath, even as others. (Eph. 2:3)

The Church is composed of forgiven sinners. There are no saints apart from the redeeming grace of God. The clean marble that God is going to use for His Temple is all taken from a very dirty quarry. The word *conversation* here simply means "way of life."

Prior to conversion, the flesh has mastery over unbelievers. The flesh is the sin principle that is woven into the very nature of our being. That was the handle that the ruler of the air used in them, and it was also that which naturally followed in the ways of the world. Before Christ, non-Christians indulge the flesh, answering its every call.

Since God is holy and the sinful nature is rebellious, there is an obvious problem. The flesh is, by its very nature, destined for destruction. It is an object of wrath. The Ephesians are described as having been children of wrath, just as the others. These others are those who are unbelievers still.

But God, who is rich in mercy, for his great love wherewith he loved us (Eph. 2:4)

So it is clear that God does what He does because He loves us. This love is not just available: it is *abundantly* available. His love for us is great. In the same way, His mercy is also abundant. God does not stingily dispense mercy with a teaspoon. Because we are greatly loved, a multitude of sins are forgiven and covered by His mercy.

Even when we were dead in sins, hath quickened us together with Christ, (by grace ye are saved) (Eph. 2:5)

Death is found in transgression. Life is found in Christ. In order to be transformed from death to life, a man must be transferred from transgression to Christ. When a man is brought to Christ, he is not "improved." He is raised to life. Good teaching cannot accomplish this any more than a nutritious meal can resurrect a corpse. Only the Spirit can make us alive with Christ. Once that has been accomplished, teaching is of course beneficial. But without that principle of life, a man is still *dead* in transgressions.

This transfer from death to life is a matter of grace. Grace is an undeserved and unmerited gift. And a gift can no more be earned than a square can be circular.

Because we have received this gift, we have been saved. The salvation received is from transgression and such salvation has natural consequences. Being dead before, we could not bring about this salvation ourselves. Consequently, it has to have been a *gift* from a merciful God.

> And hath raised us up together, and made us sit together
> in heavenly places in Christ Jesus (Eph. 2:6)

God has seen to it that Christians share in Christ's history. He died; we died in Him. He is raised, and we have been raised with Him. Apart from Christ there is no resurrection life. Another way of putting this is that we are not simply united to a static Christ. He represents us throughout the course of His entire life, from His conception to His enthronement in the heavens.

Not only do Christians share in the death and resurrection of Christ, they are also made participants in Christ's ascension and glorification. Jesus Christ is seated at the right hand of the Father now, and Christians are included in this position of glory, in Him. We are not in the heavenly realms temporarily. We are *seated* there. Because Christ is permanently there, we are permanently there.

> That in the ages to come he might shew the exceeding riches of his grace in his kindness toward us through Christ Jesus. (Eph. 2:7)

The incomparable riches of God's grace were inadequately understood at the time Paul first wrote these words. The saints of the first century could only see dimly what God had in store for the Church in the ages to come. We, two thousand years into it, have a broader view of the outworking of God's grace. It is developing, in history, and as that history progresses, God's purpose for the redemption of mankind becomes clearer and clearer. The saints who will live a thousand years from now will have an even broader vista.

With these words, Paul includes all subsequent generations of Christians in the purposive grace which God revealed in the first century. In subsequent generations, that initial deposit of grace does not dwindle away. Rather, it grows in a remarkable way because it is earning compound interest as the kingdom grows.

The leaven works through the whole loaf. The rock which struck the statue in Nebuchadnezzar's dream grows until it fills the earth. The earth will be as full of the knowledge of God as the waters cover the sea. Eyes and ears have not seen or heard what God has in store for us.

The riches of His grace that are progressively revealed in this way cannot be explained by anything in our experience. These riches are incomparable. Notice again that these great blessings do not come in the eternal state (i.e., after the general resurrection of the dead). Paul is talking about the coming ages—human history, *before* the final coming of Christ.

This grace is mediated to us because of God's kindness to us. Again, it is only found in Christ Jesus.

> For by grace are ye saved through faith; and that not of yourselves: it is the gift of God (Eph. 2:8)

Salvation is the gift that is freely offered to us. By *grace* we have been saved. Faith is the hand we extend in order to receive that gift. Faith is the sole instrument that is used to receive this gift, and it is the nature of this faith that it is entirely receptive.

Salvation does not occur when the gift is offered. It is offered to all and yet all are not saved. A man is only saved when he receives that offer by faith. Faith is the trusting attitude that agrees to receive the gift, and to receive it *as* a gift.

> For by grace are ye saved through faith; and that not of yourselves: it is the gift of God: Not of works, lest any man should boast. (Eph. 2:8–9)

As we consider verse 9, we need to back up and remind ourselves of verse 8 as the lead-in to it. We do not offer this gift to ourselves. We do not originate salvation: we only receive it. If it did begin with us, we would have a basis for boasting. But God has emphatically declared that salvation is not by human effort—it is not by works. We are the recipients of God's gift of salvation. Any belief that we can somehow deserve the gift is contrary to the Christian gospel.

Not only do we receive this grace through faith, as sheer gift, but Paul goes out of his way to note that even the ability to receive the gift (the hand of faith) is itself a gift. We are saved by grace through faith, and even that faith is a gift—so that no one might figure out a way to boast. God gives us the present, and prior to that He gives us a hand that is capable of receiving the present.

> For we are his workmanship, created in Christ Jesus unto good works, which God hath before ordained that we should walk in them. (Eph. 2:10)

We are not saved *by* our good works, obviously. But we are saved through grace *to* good works. God has created us in Christ Jesus in order that we may do good works. Faith without works is therefore dead. We are described as God's craftsmanship. The reason we do good works is that we are God's workmanship. He is the artisan and we are the project on the workbench. God's salvation enables us to work out in the world what God has already worked into us.

We don't do these works in order to become Christians. That teaching would be another gospel. But we do perform those works because we already are God's workmanship. A sheep doesn't bleat in order to become a sheep; it bleats because it is a sheep. An apple tree doesn't produce apples in order to become an apple tree; it produces apples because it already is an apple tree. When God works, we receive it as grace, and perceive it as the same. His work is to make us into new creatures, especially designed by Him to do good works. The absolute necessity of works which follow saving faith is a much neglected truth. God's salvation is made ours by faith alone. But if that faith remains alone, i.e., without works that testify to the living reality of that faith, it is not saving faith.

These works are not to be performed by us with a haphazard attitude. They are to be done with the knowledge that God has planned all of it. God has a moral agenda for our lives; it is our responsibility to trust Him to fulfill that agenda in us. He has prepared these good works beforehand so that we might walk in them.

This does not mean we must determine the will of God before we do it. It simply means we must trust Him to lead us. The fact that the Bible teaches that God has this agenda for our lives does not imply that we have the right to review that agenda beforehand. Our sole responsibility is to live it. Our lives are a mist, and without special revelation, we don't know what tomorrow will bring. But the fact that we don't know *what* good work God has planned for tomorrow must not change our availability for that work, or our ability to perform it.

> Wherefore remember, that ye being in time past Gentiles in the flesh, who are called Uncircumcision by that which is called the Circumcision in the flesh made by hands (Eph. 2:11)

The church to which Paul was writing was composed largely of those who were Gentiles by birth. They were Gentiles "in the flesh." He is reminding them that those who were circumcised Jews hold over the Gentiles the fact that they are "uncircumcised." Paul then points out the circumcision that the Jews are so proud of was merely physical. It was done to the body by men's hands. Consequently, the pride felt by "the circumcision" was not spiritually justified.

It was true that the Gentiles were separated from Christ. But that separation had nothing to do with their lack of physical circumcision. It had everything to do with the problem of sin—and that was a problem shared by circumcised Jews.

> That at that time ye were without Christ, being aliens
> from the commonwealth of Israel, and strangers from
> the covenants of promise, having no hope, and without
> God in the world (Eph. 2:12)

The Gentiles (for the most part) were not in Christ at that time, although it had nothing to do with their circumcision or lack of it. Nevertheless, they were not part of Israel and were aliens with regard to the covenant promises of God. They did not have these things because they did not have God. And without Christ, they could not enjoy citizenship in Israel and the blessing of the covenants. Without God, there is no hope. There is only despair. But when a man has God, he also has everything God has to offer.

It is important to note here that the division of Gentile/ Jew in the Old Testament was not exactly parallel to the division of unbeliever/Christian in the New. Under the new covenant, there is no other name given under Heaven by which we must be saved (Acts 4:12). Because Christ has been established as the Lord of the nations, it is necessary for all men to believe in Him and accept the mark of baptism (Matt. 28:19–20). But in the Old Testament there were numerous Gentiles who were true believers, and who had no obligation to become Jews—Melchizedek, Job, Jethro, Naaman, and numerous others. At the same time, while the two sets of categories do not map onto each other precisely, there is enough of a similarity to provide us with an analogy—which is why circumcision can be compared to baptism (Col. 2:11).

> But now in Christ Jesus ye who sometimes were far off are made nigh by the blood of Christ. (Eph. 2:13)

The gulf that separated the Gentiles from God has been closed. That reconciliation was accomplished in Christ Jesus. The nature of the solution—the blood of Christ—gives us a glimpse into the nature of the problem. The blood of Christ would not have been necessary to change Gentiles into Jews. If God can make sons of Abraham out of rocks, he can certainly do it with Gentiles. But the blood of Christ was necessary to deal with the problem of sin. So those Gentiles who believe have now been brought near to God.

> For he is our peace, who hath made both one, and hath broken down the middle wall of partition between us (Eph. 2:14)

The ethnic animosity which existed between Jew and Gentile was destroyed in Christ. In the Church, Jew and Gentile are now one. There is now a new Israel, and that Israel is found in Christ. Therefore, all who are in Christ are members of the new Israel. He is therefore the peace between Jew and Gentile because He is the new nation of the new Israel. Jesus came and was baptized as the covenantal representative of Israel and did what Israel had been unable to do throughout the course of the Old Testament, but was nevertheless obligated to do. In this new formation of Israel, the barriers excluding the Gentiles have been removed. The new has been established; the old barriers and hostilities are therefore gone.

> Having abolished in his flesh the enmity, even the law of commandments contained in ordinances; for to make in himself of twain one new man, so making peace (Eph. 2:15)

Paul is not discussing the moral law here. Love sums up the moral law, and love has not been abolished. The argument is dealing with the gulf between Jew and Gentile, which was specified by a subset within the law (commandments contained in ordinances). Christ abolished through His body the ceremonial laws and regulations which separated Jew and Gentile. He did not abolish them by setting them aside, but rather by fulfilling them. The prophetic and typological task of these laws had been accomplished and they were no longer necessary. This is the same lesson Peter learned at the house of Cornelius. What God calls clean, let no man call unclean.

So the ceremonial laws of separation were abolished, one new nation was created out of Jew and Gentile, and the body of Christ was now the basis of the peace.

> And that he might reconcile both unto God in one body
> by the cross, having slain the enmity thereby (Eph. 2:16)

Jew and Gentile are reconciled to one another only through the body of Christ. This reconciliation is accomplished through the cross, which effectively deals with sin by killing it. If the cross can remove all sin, it can certainly remove the one sin of hostility. Notice that Jew and Gentile are reconciled to God through the cross. As they are put right with Him, their animosity for one another necessarily had to cease. The primary reconciliation that has to occur is vertical—between God and man. Reconciliation between man and man is a consequent blessing, but it is a result of the other, more primary reconciliation.

> And came and preached peace to you which were afar
> off, and to them that were nigh. (Eph. 2:17)

Jesus was able to preach peace because in His body on the cross He accomplished the peace that was to be preached. This message of peace with God was preached to both Gentile and Jew—the one far away and the other near, but both separated from God. As Jew and Gentile were reconciled to God, reconciliation with the other group necessarily followed. If we walk in the light as He is in the light, *we have fellowship with one another* (1 John 1:7). It follows of necessity.

> For through him we both have access by one Spirit unto
> the Father. (Eph. 2:18)

The Jews who were near (but not near enough) were now enabled to come to the Father. The Gentiles who were far off (but not too far off) were likewise enabled to come to the Father. They both now had access to the Father. Because they have come to Him in the same way, they have become companions on the journey.

This passage contains a theology of approaching God that is thoroughly Trinitarian. A good understanding of this will affect our basic concept of how we may come to God. The direction of the Christian life is *to* the Father. We come to Him *through* the Son, Jesus Christ; Jesus Christ is our means of access. The Spirit enables us to come; we come *by* one Spirit. If we may repeat our earlier homely illustration, the Father is the destination we are traveling to, the Son is the road we take, and the Spirit is the vehicle that takes us there. We come to God, by God, in God.

> Now therefore ye are no more strangers and foreigners,
> but fellowcitizens with the saints, and of the household
> of God (Eph. 2:19)

The Father has therefore created a means for sinful men to approach Him. That means is Christ. As a result, the Gentiles have received full citizenship. There are no second-class citizens in the kingdom of God. A man is either an alien or he is a fellow citizen with the rest of God's people.

Notice that the collection of God's people is large enough to be considered as a people or nation. Members are known as citizens. Yet it is also intimate enough to be considered a household. Because of our finitude, the difference between a nation and a family cannot be reconciled in our minds. But God is great enough—it is no problem for Him. This nation is His household.

> And are built upon the foundation of the apostles and prophets, Jesus Christ himself being the chief corner stone (Eph. 2:20)

We were called a people and also a household, but here the metaphor shifts. In this verse, the people of God are considered to be a building or structure. Although the building is still under construction, the foundation has been laid once for all. God is not done with His building, although He is done with certain parts of it. The foundation is completed.

The most important part of this foundation is the cornerstone: the person and work of Jesus Christ. What He has done cannot be added to and improved. It can, however, be used as a foundation should be. As the Church continues to be built on that foundation, she testifies to its sufficiency.

The same thing is true (although to a lesser extent) of the apostles and prophets. These were men used by God to complement the cornerstone, Jesus Christ, and to complete the foundation of the Church. It is not the place of the Church to seek to duplicate the work of apostles and prophets. Rather apostolic work is foundational, while ours is ongoing. This creates the interesting question of whether the gifts of prophecy and apostleship are operative today. In the sense that Paul is using the terms here, the answer is *no*. That foundation is laid, and cannot be laid over again.

There will never be another man like the apostle Paul. There will never be another prophet like the prophet Isaiah. These men, and others like them, gave us the Old and New Testaments, which are a sufficient foundation for works of edification in the Church.

Whether there are "apostles" and "prophets" today in a weaker sense may be considered an open question, as long as none of the participants in the debate are attempting to tamper with the foundation of the Church—and any claims to special revelation from God are just such a tampering. A claim to an ability to deliver new propositional revelation from God ("thus saith the Lord") would constitute a challenge to the integrity of a completed canon of Scripture.

There is also another warning. Those who choose to use words like "apostle" and "prophet" in this weaker way should reconsider. For example, a missionary can be considered an apostle. The Greek word for *apostle* means "sent one," and missionaries *are* sent ones. As an apostle of a sending body, they have the authority of that sending body—but not an authority greater than that. So in my view it is extremely unwise to create the impression that missionaries or church leaders have apostolic authority in any biblical sense. No one today has the authority to write Scripture, and so why use terminology that creates such an impression?

> In whom all the building fitly framed together groweth
> unto an holy temple in the Lord (Eph. 2:21)

Although Christ is the foundation, His role is not limited to that. He also encompasses the entire building project. All the building is done in Him. The whole temple grows up "in the Lord."

As this building rises, its function becomes apparent. It is a holy Temple in the Lord, *for* the Lord. We, as Christians, are being pieced together as a Temple, indwelt by the Spirit of God. The Lord does not live in houses, sanctuaries, or temples made by human hands. He does live in what He is making—a Temple of living stones. He does not live in anything made *by* human hands, but it appears that He does live *in* human hands.

> In whom ye also are builded together for an habitation
> of God through the Spirit. (Eph. 2:22)

The Ephesians are included in this building, but it is not just limited to the first generation of Christians, or to that particular church. As successive generations are added, the Temple grows, as it was designed to grow. The Temple will not be complete until the roof is finally put on and the last generation of saints is firmly in place.

God lives in this Temple by means of His Holy Spirit. The Holy Spirit not only indwells believers individually, He also lives in us collectively. The Spirit dwells in the Temple.

EPHESIANS 3

THE REMARKABLE INNER MAN

In this chapter, human language almost collapses—even though it is inspired human language—under the weight of glory that God has prepared for His children. We see this at the very beginning of the chapter, where Paul starts with "I, Paul" in the nominative, and he never gets to a verb that goes with that beginning. This is no mistake in Scripture, but rather what it looks like when you put infinite glory in a finite container. This is what perfection looks like.

> For this cause I Paul, the prisoner of Jesus Christ for you Gentiles, If ye have heard of the dispensation of the grace of God which is given me to you-ward: How that

> by revelation he made known unto me the mystery; (as
> I wrote afore in few words . . . . (Eph. 3:1–21)

Like a magnifying glass focusing a sunbeam on one burning spot, the glories described in the first two chapters now come down to the ministry of Paul, a prisoner for the sake of the Gentiles (v. 1). He was given the administration of God's grace to the Gentiles (v. 2). An unveiled mystery had been given to Paul by revelation, which he had written about previously (v. 3). This might refer to a previous letter, or it might refer to the first two chapters of this epistle. He calls what he had written "the mystery of Christ," and if the Ephesians read it, they will understand Paul's knowledge of it. Previous ages did not know this, but the Spirit has now revealed it to the apostles and prophets (v. 5). That mystery was that the Gentiles were to be fully included in all the promises (v. 6). Paul was given this mystery and was made a minister of this mystery (v. 7). He was not worthy of the honor, but was given the tremendous privilege of preaching the unsearchable riches of Christ to the Gentiles anyway (v. 8). This would make all men see the nature of this *fellowship*, which was the whole point from the very first (v. 9). When this happened, then even the principalities and powers in the heavenly places would see the manifold wisdom of God (v. 10). This was His eternal purpose in Christ (v. 11).

This being the case, we have boldness in our access through faith into His presence (v. 12). This puts tribulation for Christ's sake into a completely different light—it is glory (v. 13). This is why Paul bows the knee before the Father

(v. 14), from whom all fatherhood derives its name (v. 15). Paul asks that God would grant, according to His riches, that we—I include us with the Ephesians here (v. 18)—be strengthened by the Spirit in the inner man (v. 16), in order that Christ might dwell in us by faith, rooting us deeply in His love (v. 17), and that we might be able to comprehend the incomprehensible (v. 18), to know the unknowable (v. 19), and to be filled with *all* the fullness of God (v. 19). And if that were not enough, Paul asks the benediction in the name of the one who can do a whole lot more than *that* (v. 20)—and may He have glory in the Church, through Christ Jesus, unto a piled-up eternity of ages (v. 21). And then he says *amen* to all of *that* (v. 21).

God is the unfolder of great surprises. What He continually does is invite us to take a step back and use the "zoom out" feature. Now, see? We thought the task of the godly was to keep our candle lit in a blustery night. The candle was all the purposes of God, and the surrounding windy night was the inexorable power of worldliness. But zoom out. The sun is rising. The night is done, gone, over. Christ has risen, and He will never set. The time of night is long past, and so Christians ought to quit seeking out dark corners of basements in order be able to play their pessimistic game of "night time." The first great move was from Jew to Jew and Gentile together. The next was Christian and unbeliever. Just as Gentiles came into Israel through Christ, so also unbelievers will come into Christ . . . through Christ.

This section of Scripture does not just contain big words, but rather *immense* words. He refers to the "unsearchable riches" of Christ (v. 8). He wants all men to see what God hid from the beginning of the world (v. 9). He wants crushed glory here to be bold before the throne of God (vv. 12–13). Notice the juxtaposition of "boldness" and "bow." He wants us to be strengthened with *might*, according to *His* riches, not according to our capacity (v. 16). He wants us to comprehend, along with all the saints, the length, breadth, depth, and height (v. 18). He wants us to know what can't be known (v. 19). He wants us to be filled with the fullness of God (v. 19), and he wants us to learn how to think of all these things as the first page of the first chapter of the first book in a library filled with an infinite number of volumes. Think of this. Christ is always the infinite wisdom of God, and you, by His grace, are going to live forever.

In verse 16, Paul speaks of the inner man being strengthened with might by the Holy Spirit. The strengthening of this inner man is such that all the staggering gifts in the verses that follow might become possible. This inner man is *not* referring to the soul as opposed to the body, and it is not contrasting the innards with the epidermis. Paul here is speaking of the regenerate man—the man within that has been brought to life. He is speaking of the new heart, the principle of new life which is able to "get" what he is talking about here. He speaks the same way in 2 Corinthians 4:16–17:

> For which cause we faint not; but though our outward man perish, yet the inward man is renewed day by day. For our light affliction, which is but for a moment, worketh for us a far more exceeding and eternal weight of glory.

This is the same thing. Being born again is not just becoming a nice person instead of a nasty one (although that is involved). Being born again means being fitted out for glory, and the tribulations you go through now are simply God's way of stress-testing the rivets.

VERSE BY VERSE

In this third chapter, Paul is exulting in the culmination of God's purposes for human history, which, as we saw in the previous chapter, was the making of one new man out of two (2:15). Where there had once between Jew and Gentile, there is now the new man—the Christian. This glorifies God in the Church by Christ Jesus, throughout all ages (3:21).

> For this cause I Paul, the prisoner of Jesus Christ for you Gentiles (Eph. 3:1)

Paul wrote this epistle from prison. He was there for two reasons. One, he was in a human prison because he had already been taken captive by Christ. The jails of this world have held many for the same reason. Captives of Christ are frequently taken captive by men. Secondly, Paul was there for the sake of the Gentiles. The Jews were not hostile to Paul because he thought Jesus was the Messiah. They were hostile because he believed Jesus was the Messiah who came for the salvation of all men, including the Gentiles as Gentiles. He was the Christ for Gentiles who were under no subsequent responsibility to become Jews.

> If ye have heard of the dispensation of the grace of God
> which is given me to you-ward (Eph. 3:2)

The Gentiles in Ephesus were by no means unaware of Paul's responsibility from God in preaching to them. God's message of grace was for everyone, Jew and Gentile alike. Paul had come to them because God had equipped and commissioned him to do so.

> How that by revelation he made known unto me the
> mystery; (as I wrote afore in few words (Eph. 3:3)

The mystery Paul speaks of here is not a mystery concealed, but rather a mystery revealed. It is called a mystery because at one time it was hidden. But now through divine revelation, the mystery is entirely disclosed.

Paul mentions that he has already written on this briefly. Either he is referring to an earlier letter, now lost to us, or he is speaking of the first two chapters of Ephesians. Because of the way he expresses it, it seems the latter option is the more likely.

> Whereby, when ye read, ye may understand my knowl-
> edge in the mystery of Christ) (Eph. 3:4)

In reading what Paul has to say, we will not only understand the content of the mystery but also how Paul came to possess the insight. His insight was made possible for him by God's revelation. It did not originate with Paul. Paul was given the understanding of it, which he then communicated to others.

> Which in other ages was not made known unto the sons
> of men, as it is now revealed unto his holy apostles and
> prophets by the Spirit (Eph. 3:5)

This mystery of Christ was revealed by means of the Holy Spirit to the apostles and prophets. The word *prophets* here cannot refer to the prophets of the Old Testament era because the verse clearly states that it was not made known to previous generations. God's grand intention has now been fully disclosed.

> That the Gentiles should be fellowheirs, and of the
> same body, and partakers of his promise in Christ by
> the gospel (Eph. 3:6)

The mystery is not at all complex. It may have been emotionally difficult for first-century Jews to accept, but it was not logically difficult. The mystery was that Gentiles were to be fully included in the promise in Christ Jesus. This is stated three ways here. Gentiles are (1) heirs together with the Jews; (2) members along with the Jews of one body; (3) sharers with the Jews in the promise.

So according to the teaching of the New Testament, there is only one real Israel, and believing Jews and believing Gentiles together comprise that true Israel. Unbelieving descendants of Abraham have no part in this true Israel. The "chosen people" are no longer to be identified ethnically. God can make sons of Abraham out of rocks. There is only one Israel, and that Israel is the body of Christ.

> Whereof I was made a minister, according to the gift of
> the grace of God given unto me by the effectual work-
> ing of his power. (Eph. 3:7)

When God first called Paul to serve this gospel he was vio-
lently headed in the opposite direction. It was God's gift and
God's power that turned him around and made Paul's service possible. The initiation belonged to God, the response
to Paul. In no way did Paul earn this gift. If he had, the gift
would no longer be a gift, and grace no longer grace. Prior
to conversion, Paul had no power to change directions.
When God intervened with this power gift, Paul accepted it.
He was not disobedient to the heavenly vision, as he put it
in the book of Acts (26:19).

> Unto me, who am less than the least of all saints, is this
> grace given, that I should preach among the Gentiles
> the unsearchable riches of Christ (Eph. 3:8)

Paul probably considered himself least in the Church
of God because of his former persecution of Christians.
He knew very clearly that far from earning a place in the
Church, he had viciously attacked it. Nevertheless, God
gave him this grace—to preach the Christian gospel. The
mission field assigned to Paul was the Gentile world. The
message was the unsearchable riches of Christ. Notice that
the message was a person—Christ. Not only that, but it
was a message of a Christ with no limitations—a message
of unsearchable riches. The Christian preacher proclaims a
person whose wealth, riches, and resources are infinite.

> And to make all men see what is the fellowship of the
> mystery, which from the beginning of the world hath
> been hid in God, who created all things by Jesus Christ
> (Eph. 3:9)

Paul's job was to preach the mystery, and also to make it plain to everyone. He was to set out and make clear how this revealed mystery was being administered by God. In the past centuries this mystery had been closed up in the heart of the Creator God. It has now been made manifest.

> To the intent that now unto the principalities and pow-
> ers in heavenly places might be known by the church
> the manifold wisdom of God (Eph. 3:10)

What was God's purpose in the long concealment? His intention was to use the Church as a demonstration of His wisdom. The wisdom had many facets and God wanted to make it known to the rulers and authorities in the heavens. These rulers and authorities are most likely the same rulers and authorities as we will find in chapter 6, and against whom the spiritual war is being fought. The Church, as God and these celestial authorities see it, is a clear statement of God's vindicating wisdom.

> According to the eternal purpose which he purposed in
> Christ Jesus our Lord (Eph. 3:11)

This display of wisdom was intended by God from all eternity. There was no last-minute change of plans, no confusion in the mind of God. This purpose, the creation of the Church and all that entails, was accomplished in Christ Jesus. The Church is the Church because she is in Christ, her Lord.

> In whom we have boldness and access with confidence
> by the faith of him. (Eph. 3:12)

Again, we approach God the Father through and in Jesus Christ. Jesus is the way to the Father. We take advantage of this means to the Father through faith—our faith in Christ. The result is that we approach God with freedom and confidence. If I am at the door of any house but my own, I knock. This is because I don't know if I am welcome at that time. But with my own house, I have freedom and confidence. It is the same here. Because of Jesus Christ, the Christian need have no hesitation when he approaches the Father. If hesitation exists, then the individual is either not genuinely a Christian, or else is a Christian with a very inadequate understanding of what Jesus came to do.

> Wherefore I desire that ye faint not at my tribulations
> for you, which is your glory. (Eph. 3:13)

Because all these things are so in the heavenly realm, nothing that happens down here should discourage the believer. Consequently, Paul asks the Ephesians not to be discouraged on his behalf. His sufferings, far from being a shame to him, are a glory. The Ephesians should embrace them as their glory.

> For this cause I bow my knees unto the Father of our
> Lord Jesus Christ (Eph. 3:14)

This word *therefore* ties in with what Paul has said before. Paul is humbled by what God has done for us in Christ. As a result, he prays to the Father. Again, we may see the central place occupied by the Father in a biblical understanding of prayer. Notice also Paul's posture in prayer—he kneels. Kneeling in prayer is helpful for a couple reasons. One, it keeps the mind from wandering. Kneeling is an uncomfortable position and can help keep the mind concentrated. Secondly, it is a humble position. It is difficult to maintain an arrogant or haughty spirit when you are kneeling before the Father of our Lord.

> Of whom the whole family in heaven and earth is
> named (Eph. 3:15)

At the core of all that is, there is a *Father*. A better rendering here would be "from whom all fatherhood is named." All earthly fathers and whatever heavenly fathers exist draw their name from the one Father. They are fathers because they reflect, however dimly, something of Him.

We do not call God our Father because we have earthly fathers. It is quite the reverse. He does not derive His name from us; we derive our names from Him.

> That he would grant you, according to the riches of his
> glory, to be strengthened with might by his Spirit in the
> inner man (Eph. 3:16)

Again, Paul states his prayer for the Ephesians. The object of his prayer is that they be powerfully strengthened in their inner being. This strengthening would be done by means of the Holy Spirit of God, the Spirit who indwells believers.

The doctrine of grace is clearly seen in that the strengthening is done according to God's glorious riches, and not according to our miserable poverty.

> That Christ may dwell in your hearts by faith; that ye, being rooted and grounded in love (Eph. 3:17)

The result of this strengthening is the dwelling of Christ in their hearts through faith. Think of Christ settling in, making Himself at home in the heart of someone who is already a believer. The reality is experienced by faith. The Christian life is a life of faith from first to last (Rom. 1:17).

Paul continues his prayer by expressing a desire that the Ephesians be rooted and grounded in love. This does not mean a superficial, surface contact with love. Just as roots penetrate soil and cause a tree to be established firmly, so the Christian's roots should go deep into love. This love is not an emotional state. The Bible defines love in terms of obedience, a willing obedience that comes from the heart. Paul wants the Ephesians to be rooted firmly in love—a love that expresses itself in joyful obedience to the commands of God.

> May be able to comprehend with all saints what is the breadth, and length, and depth, and height (Eph. 3:18)

Paul wants them to have a grasp of the ungraspable. The love of Christ is not something that can be properly understood unless God grants the understanding. What Paul wants them to understand is the extent of Christ's love—how wide, deep, long, and high it is. Because God is God, that extent is infinite.

This is something Paul wants all the saints to comprehend. It is not a truth tailored for some spiritual elite. All Christians should be able to grasp an understanding of this love. This ability is explained by the grace of God, not by innate competence on the part of believers.

> And to know the love of Christ, which passeth knowledge, that ye might be filled with all the fulness of God.
> (Eph. 3:19)

Paul moves on in order to pray that the Ephesians might come to know the unknowable. He qualifies his statement by saying he means for them to be filled with all God's fullness. This is like praying for a glass of water to be able to contain the Pacific Ocean, and Paul understands that this is the kind of thing he is praying for. Paul prays that finite beings be able to contain the fullness of an infinite Being. How God accomplishes this we will see shortly (Eph. 4:10–13).

> Now unto him that is able to do exceeding abundantly above all that we ask or think, according to the power that worketh in us (Eph. 3:20)

These things which are impossible for man are possible for God. Paul closes this section with a benediction, addressed to the only One who is able to do so much with creatures like us. In our own wisdom and strength, we cannot pray for, or even imagine, the sorts of things Paul prayed for in the previous sentence. Paul's prayer, however, was addressed to God, not man.

The answer to the prayer is accomplished, as always, according to God's power, not according to ours. On the other hand, Paul says the power is at work within us. To say that God does this work does not place the work far away from us. To say that the work is done within us is not to say that believers are the ones doing it. God, in His grace, has consented to work in the lives of all saints. He does that which is impossible for us to conceive or do on our own.

> Unto him be glory in the church by Christ Jesus through-
> out all ages, world without end. Amen. (Eph. 3:21)

Because God is the one who accomplishes this, the glory and praise for it are to go to Him. This glorification occurs in the Church and in Christ Jesus. What God has established in the Church will never cease and consequently the praise will never cease. It will go on through all generations, for-ever and ever. This fact reminds us that God's purpose for the Church was not limited to the first century. He intends for His glory to be evident in the Church and in Christ throughout all generations. We learn elsewhere that this glory becomes progressively manifest.

Paul concludes with a call to his readers to join with him in his hope and prayer when he finishes with *amen*.

EPHESIANS 4

PUTTING ON THE JESUS COAT

Adam was created in the image of God (Gen. 1:27). After the disastrous fall into sin, mankind retained the image of God (Gen. 9:6), but it was barely recognizable, lying now in ruins. The purpose of Christ coming was to re-establish mankind in the second Adam, and to renew the image of God in us. This is why we are told in this chapter to put off the old man, to be renewed, and to put on the new man. That image is described for us here (v. 24), created in the likeness of God as righteousness and true holiness.

> I therefore, the prisoner of the Lord, beseech you that
> ye walk worthy of the vocation wherewith ye are called,
> With all lowliness and meekness, with longsuffering,

forbearing one another in love; Endeavouring to keep the
unity of the Spirit in the bond of peace . . . . (Eph. 4:1–32)

Paul reminds them again that he is a prisoner, and asks
them to walk worthily of the calling he has just been describing for them (v. 1). What does that look like? In a word, it
looks like humility (v. 2). Such humility is the foundation
for the strenuous labor of church unity (v. 3). That unity is
grounded in what God has done—one body, one Spirit, one
hope, one Lord, one faith, one baptism, and one God over
all, through all, and in you all (vv. 4–6). We all have that in
common. All believers, by definition, share that.

But to each Christian a particular grace is given (v. 7).
Paul refers to the Ascension, after which Christ bestowed
gifts on us (v. 8). But before He ascended He had to first
go down (v. 9). The one who descended is the same one
who ascended (v. 10). The gifts He gave (as listed here)
are apostles, prophets, evangelists, and pastors/teachers
(v. 11). These gifts were to equip the saints for the work of
ministry, not to put on a hired show for the spectators (v.
12). These gifts will be exercised until we all arrive at the
unity of the faith, to the perfect man (v. 13). At that time,
we will no longer be gullible, the prey of false teachers (v.
14). Rather, we will speak the truth in love, which shows
attachment to the head, who is Christ (v. 15). The entire
body is connected to Him, and love is what makes it all
grow (v. 16).

That being the case, Christians ought not to walk according to the Gentile mindset (v. 17). Their problem is intellectual darkness created by heart blindness. When the heart is

blind, the head is dark (v. 18). Their intellectual darkness not surprisingly is connected to moral corruption (v. 19). But the Ephesians had not learned Christ in that way (v. 20), at least not if they had heard the real Jesus and been taught by Him (v. 21). They had been taught to seize the old man, the old way of life, and take him off (v. 22). Then they were to be renewed in the spirit of their mind (v. 23) and put on the new man, who is of course Jesus Christ Himself (v. 24). In this place we are being reminded to continue to put on our Jesus coat.

A cluster of ethical instructions then follow. Stop lying, and speak the truth to one another (v. 25). Be angry, but don't sin, and don't let it fester (v. 26). Don't give the devil a place; don't let him have a foothold (v. 27). Let the thief work with his hands on something and share what he has earned with others (v. 28). Don't speak in a foul way (v. 29). Do not grieve the Spirit (v. 30). Put away malice and all its companions (v. 31). Be kind to each other, tender-hearted, eager to forgive as you have been forgiven (v. 32). Don't stand there as a spiritual leper, with little pieces of damnation falling off.

There are two kinds of unity in this chapter, and we can see an already/not yet sort of unity in it. The first is a gift from God, and it is a unity that needs to be protected and retained. We are told to *keep* the unity of the Spirit. In order to keep it, we have to already have it. This is a natural consequence of regeneration. Those who are part of the one true body of Christ have already, as a gift, true unity with one another. This is why a Baptist and a Presbyterian, belonging to different churches, can have true unity with one another.

This kind of unity is disrupted by arrogance, by a lack of humility. This is why two Presbyterians, members of the same church, can be at one another's throats. When this kind of unity is disrupted, it is *always* because of sin.

The second kind of unity is what we are all growing toward. This unity cannot be preserved because we are not there yet. This is what Paul refers to in verse 13, when he says that we will eventually come to "the unity of the faith," or, put another way, to "a perfect man." The lack of this kind of unity is not a sin, and not a problem. God governs human history, not us.

Look at a fertilized egg under a microscope, a person who will be a mature man thirty-five years from now. What you see is perfect unity. What is the first step toward the higher unity of the perfect man? The answer is division. Look at Adam before he met Eve. What do you see? You see unity. What was the first step in creating the higher unity of a human race of billions of people? The answer was division. We shouldn't try to tell God how to govern Church history. But we should receive what He tells us about *our* demeanor in our particular corner of Church history.

What does that mean? In verse 30, we are told not to grieve the Holy Spirit. At the beginning of the chapter, we are told to keep the unity of the Spirit (v. 3). We are told that there is one body and one Spirit (v. 4). The way we keep the unity of the Spirit is by humility—lowliness, meekness, patience, etc. The way we grieve the Spirit is by bitterness, wrath, anger, clamor, evil-speaking, and malice (v. 31).

Humility and love help the body to grow. Anger, clamor, and dissension do not. Keep what God has given. Do not

grasp after what He has not yet given. To grasp after the
second kind of unity prematurely is to replicate the sin of
Adam and Eve at the tree. They wanted what had not been
given to them *yet*. Those who strive for the second kind of
unity almost always trample the first kind. Those who cultivate the first kind are being used by God in His glorious
eschatological purposes.

VERSE BY VERSE

The beginning of this chapter is where Paul turns from laying the foundation stones of his grand indicatives and begins
his course of ethical instruction, his imperatives. The first
three chapters have been telling us what *is* so. The last three
chapters instruct us how those people who have believed
the first three chapters should behave—what *should* be so.

> I therefore, the prisoner of the Lord, beseech you that
> ye walk worthy of the vocation wherewith ye are called
> (Eph. 4:1)

Paul has spent the first part of the book establishing the
doctrinal basis for the Christian life. At this point in the letter, he begins urging the Ephesians to begin building on that
foundation or base in practical ways. As a prisoner for the
sake of Christ, Paul urges the Ephesians to *live* in a certain
way. He reminds them of the calling they received—their
position in Christ that he discussed in the first part of the
letter—and exhorts them to live in a fashion that is consistent with that truth.

The ethical imperatives that fill the latter half of the book presuppose an understanding of the doctrinal indicative statements in the first half. The hinge of the epistle is the second word of this verse—*therefore*. Given everything that has been taught in the first half, believers should *therefore* live a certain way.

> With all lowliness and meekness, with longsuffering, forbearing one another in love (Eph. 4:2)

Humility is the attitude of putting the interests of others first. It is not the same thing as cultivating a "low self-image." Someone could have a low opinion of himself and still be self-centered. Humility is when the self is not center stage. One who is arrogant and conceited is not humble; neither is someone who is depressed and self-absorbed. In both cases, the individual is putting himself first. Paul forbids this by commanding the Ephesians to be completely humble.

Gentleness is not coarse, abrasive, or domineering. Neither does Paul want Christians to be.

They are told to bear with one another in love. It is possible to bear with someone in an unloving manner—but such an attitude is not patience. If we put up with someone, but in an irritated manner, it is not patience. It is only patience if it is done in love, love from the inside out.

> Endeavouring to keep the unity of the Spirit in the bond of peace. (Eph. 4:3)

The Ephesians are not instructed here to *create* the unity of the Spirit. They are instructed to preserve something that has already been created and given to them. The Spirit has already unified believers. The believers are instructed to make every effort to keep or preserve that unity.

To understand this passage as a basis for the modern ecumenical movement is a mistake on two counts. First, Paul is talking about a unity between individuals united in a common faith. This unity is characterized by humility, gentleness, patience, and love. He is not talking about unity between various organizations or institutions—an organizational unity.

Secondly, he is talking about unity between believers. The modern ecumenical movement establishes an unequal yoke between believers and unbelievers.

True Christians are to recognize and maintain the unity that the Spirit has established. They are not to attempt to manufacture their own. To do so is to forget the centrality of the Spirit's work in the formation of the Church.

> There is one body, and one Spirit, even as ye are called
> in one hope of your calling (Eph. 4:4)

There is only one body and only one Spirit. Jesus Christ has only one bride: He is not a polygamist. Paul teaches us in 1 Corinthians 12:13 that we were all baptized into that one body by the one Spirit. That body is the body of Christ, and it is not synonymous with any human denomination. It consists of all those who have been born again due to the regenerative power of the Holy Spirit.

True Christians are therefore united by a common hope—the hope that our final salvation will be revealed from the heavens when Jesus Christ returns. Christians were called to that hope when they were first called to be Christians.

Local Christian churches and fellowships should strive to maintain the unity of the Spirit with fellow believers who are outside their particular gathering. Our standards for fellowship should not be higher than God's.

One Lord, one faith, one baptism (Eph. 4:5)

Those who serve different lords belong to different faiths. Those who serve the same Lord are united in one faith. This unity is centered on the person of Jesus Christ and His attributes, and not on the name alone. Many cults lift up the "name" of Jesus while denying His character that He has revealed to us. In such a situation, unity is not possible. Unity occurs when people have a common faith (one faith) in a common Lord (one Lord).

This faith is expressed outwardly in water baptism. Baptism is divisive when it is seen as a doorway into human institutions and denominations. It is a unifying factor if it represents to the person baptized his unity with Christ in His death and resurrection. As such, it belongs to all Christians together. Those who have one Lord and one faith also have one baptism.

One God and Father of all, who is above all, and through all, and in you all. (Eph. 4:6)

Everything flows from the Father and everything returns to Him.

According to Paul, there is one faith because there is one God. That this God is personal can be seen from Paul's use of the words "Father of all." This God is transcendent and sovereign. He stands apart from and rules over His creation. He is "over all." Although transcendent, He is not divorced from the creation as can be seen from the expression "through all, and in you all." Paul's doctrine thus stands in distinction from Deism on the one hand and Pantheism on the other.

> But unto every one of us is given grace according to the measure of the gift of Christ. (Eph. 4:7)

Grace has not been given only to a few; it has been given to each one in the body. The grace has been apportioned by Christ, not by us. The recipients of His grace do not determine how that grace is to be distributed.

> Wherefore he saith, When he ascended up on high, he led captivity captive, and gave gifts unto men. (Eph. 4:8)

The quotation is from Psalm 68:18. Paul applies this exalted language to Jesus Christ. The point of the citation appears to be twofold. One, Christ's ascension into the heavens is seen as an ascension of triumph, similar in kind to Yahweh's ascension of Mt. Zion in the establishment of His sanctuary there. Two, this ascension precedes the giving of gifts to the people—which seems to be Paul's main point.

Some have thought Paul misapplied the psalm because he quotes it as saying "gave gifts" where the Old Testament reads "received gifts." The difficulty appears larger than it actually is. Any conquering king will both receive tribute from his enemies and distribute gifts to his people. This concept is seen in Acts 2:33 where it is said, "Exalted to the right hand of God, He has received from the Father the promised Holy Spirit and has poured out what you now see and hear." Christ gives what He has received. Paul is not making up a concept out of whole cloth. Several ancient versions (Aramaic and Syriac) render the psalm the same way Paul does.

(Now that he ascended, what is it but that he also descended first into the lower parts of the earth? (Eph. 4:9)

In order to go up, Jesus must have first been down. In order to ascend, He must have first descended. Before He is exalted above every name, He first humbles Himself.

There has been some debate over what is meant by the "lower earthy regions." Some have held that this refers to the "harrowing of hell"—that is, the descent of Christ into Hades between the cross and the resurrection. Others have held that it refers to the Incarnation—the Word descending to become man. I believe that latter interpretation fits in with Paul's argument more consistently. To say this, however, is not to deny the first doctrine. The Bible clearly teaches elsewhere that Christ descended into Hades. For example, in Psalm 16:10, the Messiah is promised that He will not be abandoned to Sheol. This verse is quoted in Acts 2:27, applied to Christ, and the Hebrew *Sheol* is translated as *Hades*. Christ died and went to Hades, as the Creed says, but was not abandoned there. The question is simply whether that truth is being referred to here.

> He that descended is the same also that ascended up
> far above all heavens, that he might fill all things.)
> (Eph. 4:10)

The exalted Christ is not to be distinguished from Jesus
of Nazareth. The one who ascended is the same one who
descended. This Christ has ascended higher than all the
heavens. There is nothing above Him (except God the
Father—1 Cor. 15:27). He is now the fullness of everything
in the universe.

> And he gave some, apostles; and some, prophets; and
> some, evangelists; and some, pastors and teachers
> (Eph. 4:11)

Christ, when He gave the Holy Spirit, also gave the gifts
that come from Him. In this list, four gifts or offices are mentioned: apostle, prophet, evangelist, and pastor/teacher.

Two of the gifts have to do with laying the foundation,
and the other two have to do with building on that foundation. The foundation offices are apostle and prophet, and
they have been discussed in the notes earlier (Eph. 2:20).
We have the results of that ministry in the Scriptures.

The latter offices have an ongoing nature. The foundation
has been laid, once for all, but the house is not yet complete.
Until the day of completion, there will be work for evangelists and pastors/teachers to do. Those who function in these
offices are responsible for two basic areas—birth and growth.

The evangelist, in bringing people to Christ, is responsible for birth. He is a spiritual midwife. The pastor/teacher,

in instructing them, is responsible for growth. To return to the building metaphor, the evangelist brings new material to the site, and the pastor/teacher fits it into the building. The evangelist is the lumberjack, and the pastor/teacher is the contractor.

> For the perfecting of the saints, for the work of the ministry, for the edifying of the body of Christ (Eph. 4:12)

These gifts were not given to the body so that a few people would then do all the work. The work is done by all God's people. The evangelist and the pastor/teacher, using the words of the apostles and prophets, equip the people of God for the work that they must do.

Where this pattern exists, the body of Christ is built up. To *edify* simply means to build. To be an edifice means to have *been* built. It does not exist when the evangelists or pastors/teachers take all the work upon themselves out of a sense of self-importance. Neither does it exist when the ordinary Christian refuses to be equipped out of laziness.

> Till we all come in the unity of the faith, and of the knowledge of the Son of God, unto a perfect man, unto the measure of the stature of the fulness of Christ (Eph. 4:13)

The two goals of this process of "building up" are unity and maturity. In both areas, the goal is understood in both a present and a future sense. In verse 3 of this chapter, the

Ephesians are told to *keep* the unity of the Spirit. Yet here a complete unity is seen as something not fully attained.

In a similar way, maturity is both present and future. It is possible to be mature and yet grow in maturity. It is possible to be unified and yet grow in unity. When these goals are realized, the Church will have attained to all the fullness Christ has to offer.

> That we henceforth be no more children, tossed to and fro, and carried about with every wind of doctrine, by the sleight of men, and cunning craftiness, whereby they lie in wait to deceive (Eph. 4:14)

The result of this type of ministry is unity and maturity. One consequence of this is the ability to resist false teaching. Notice that the protection from false teaching is afforded because of stability. People who are tossed back and forth, as if by waves, or blown about, as if by wind, are people who are vulnerable to false doctrine. They are vulnerable because of instability.

If evangelistic and teaching gifts are exercised as they ought to be in the body, the result will be stability, i.e., the saints will know what they believe and why they believe it, and they will hold to it in love.

> But speaking the truth in love, may grow up into him in all things, which is the head, even Christ (Eph. 4:15)

Contrasted to instability is the ability to speak the truth lovingly. Truth without love is harsh and unyielding—and ultimately ceases to be truth. Love without truth is soft and accommodating—but ultimately ceases to be love. The biblical balance includes the two.

Speaking the truth lovingly characterizes those who are growing up into their head, Jesus Christ. This growth is not limited to certain areas; it includes all things.

> From whom the whole body fitly joined together and compacted by that which every joint supplieth, according to the effectual working in the measure of every part, maketh increase of the body unto the edifying of itself in love. (Eph. 4:16)

The ultimate source of this building and growth is the head. It is not a growth of autonomous Christians united to the head but separate from each other. Rather, those who are joined to the head are also joined to each other. This lack of autonomy means that growth has to occur in the context of love.

While the growth originates with the head, and certain gifts are used to facilitate that growth, it is still necessary for each part to do its work. No part of the body may sit back and say, "I am not needed."

> This I say therefore, and testify in the Lord, that ye henceforth walk not as other Gentiles walk, in the vanity of their mind (Eph. 4:17)

The maturity of Christian thinking is contrasted with that of the non-Christian Gentiles. The Ephesians' thinking is to be stable and mature, not futile. Paul is not making a suggestion. He insists that intellectual futility be avoided.

Worldly "wisdom" is rejected because it is worldly, and not because it is "wise." Man's wisdom is foolishness to God. Ungodly intellectualism may be clever, urbane, or sophisticated. But at bottom, it is always futile, and Christians must avoid it.

Reason has an important place in the Christian's life, but it is a subservient role. It is not the protector; it is the thing protected. I do not wear the helmet of reason in order to protect my godliness. I must wear the helmet of godliness in order to protect my reason.

> Having the understanding darkened, being alienated from the life of God through the ignorance that is in them, because of the blindness of their heart (Eph. 4:18)

Paul's teaching is that intellectual darkness is a consequence of moral depravity. The point here is that hard hearts become ignorant hearts. This ignorance then has two results—separation from the life of God (spiritual death) and separation from the mind of God (intellectual darkness).

This same point is made elsewhere. In Colossians 1:21, it says, "Once you were alienated from God and were enemies in your minds because of your evil behavior." Immorality leads to intellectual hostility toward God. In Romans 1:21, a refusal to glorify God or thank Him plunges the fool into intellectual darkness.

The unbeliever does not ask questions in order to receive the truth. He asks them to keep the truth away. To receive the truth requires repentance from immorality.

> Who being past feeling have given themselves over unto lasciviousness, to work all uncleanness with greediness. (Eph. 4:19)

When the heart is hard, moral sensitivity is lost. The conscience is seared and can no longer protect the individual from the destructiveness of sin. Just as nerve endings warn us of physical destruction, so a conscience warns us of sin. But when the heart is hard, there is nothing to prevent the individual from destroying himself. Every kind of impure pleasure is experienced, but the continual presence of lust indicates there is no satisfaction.

> But ye have not so learned Christ (Eph. 4:20)

Paul reminds the Ephesians that when they first heard the gospel, it represented a sharp break with their past. Their knowledge of Christ was not gained in the context of immorality. It represented a moral difference.

> If so be that ye have heard him, and have been taught by him, as the truth is in Jesus (Eph. 4:21)

The message they heard and the truth they were taught were consistent with the character of Jesus Christ. The practices of the pagans were rejected on the basis of the holiness of Christ. The message of Christianity is Christ. Nothing may be retained if it is inconsistent with His character.

> That ye put off concerning the former conversation the old man, which is corrupt according to the deceitful lusts (Eph. 4:22)

Remember that *conversation* here simply means "way of life." When the Ephesians were evangelized, they were taught to break with their past. They were taught how deceitful desires were corrupting them. Their hearts were hard; they were spiritually dead. Their minds were trapped in futility. They were told to reject all that futility when they received Christ. They were told to put off the old self.

Paul is not telling the Ephesians, as Christians, to put off the old self. He is not telling them to do something; he is reminding them of what they had been taught when they were first evangelized. They should continue to live as though they had been taught that way from the first.

> And be renewed in the spirit of your mind (Eph. 4:23)

At that time, the Ephesians were taught that Christianity involved a completely different mental attitude. Notice that Christians are "made new"; they do not make themselves new. God is the one who renews. Nevertheless, the Christian has a responsibility in the process—he is taught to be made new.

> And that ye put on the new man, which after God is created in righteousness and true holiness. (Eph. 4:24)

At conversion, the Ephesians were instructed to replace the old self with the new. They were not told to maintain both side by side. When the new comes, the old must go. The old man is dead and has no residual authority, however powerful he may seem.

The new nature is designed by God to be righteous and holy. It is created by God to be like God. Consequently, Christians have no affinity with the world and its ways. The old self is gone. It is now normal for Christians to be righteous and holy, just as God is. This is not because Christians are worthy, but because God is gracious.

> Wherefore putting away lying, speak every man truth with his neighbour: for we are members one of another. (Eph. 4:25)

Because the old nature was put off in the past, certain activities must be rejected in the present. Falsehood and lying to one's neighbor are inconsistent with the new life that Christ offers.

Because Christians are united in one body, that unity should not be strained with hypocrisy and lies. For followers of the truth, speaking the truth should be characteristic of all relationships between members of that body.

> Be ye angry, and sin not: let not the sun go down upon your wrath: Neither give place to the devil. (Eph. 4:26–27)

The quotation is from Psalm 4:4. This is a command to be angry, and not a recognition that Christians sometimes happen to get angry. There are many evils which require a godly anger in response. The fact that it is difficult to keep our anger within God's boundaries should not keep us from obeying this command. It is also difficult to keep our love within His boundaries. Nevertheless, love is still expected of us.

Man's selfish anger does not accomplish what God desires (James 1:20), but neither does man's refusal to get angry when God requires it.

But even when the anger is righteous, it should be temporary. Even a godly anger will turn to bitterness if we let the sun go down on it. It is like manna and will go rancid overnight. When Jesus was angry, the result was constructive; a man's hand was healed (Mark 3:5). If our anger does not accomplish something before sundown, then we should let it go. Otherwise the devil will get a foothold and can make us bitter and resentful.

> Let him that stole steal no more: but rather let him labour, working with his hands the thing which is good, that he may have to give to him that needeth. (Eph. 4:28)

The only alternative to theft is work. Paul commands those who are thieves to begin productive lives. Stealing is inconsistent with the law of love; work is not.

The work must not be busy work; it must be truly productive. If the former thief is productive, he will be in a position to help minister to the needy. He will then help keep *them* from the temptation of stealing.

> Let no corrupt communication proceed out of your
> mouth, but that which is good to the use of edifying,
> that it may minister grace unto the hearers. (Eph. 4:29)

Unhealthy, unwholesome talk should not be heard from a Christian. Paul here defines unwholesome talk in terms of its impact. Wholesome speech is speech which builds up or edifies the hearer.

The listener should be strengthened in the area of his need. The speaker is responsible to determine what that area is and speak to it. The result is beneficial to the listener. Avoid quarrels, slander, gossip, and the like. They can only tear down the hearer, not build him up.

> And grieve not the holy Spirit of God, whereby ye are
> sealed unto the day of redemption. (Eph. 4:30)

That the Holy Spirit is a person can be clearly seen in the fact that He can be grieved. He is not an impersonal force. He is an eternal person, able to be grieved by our sinful behavior.

The day of redemption is the day of resurrection when Jesus returns. We have been sealed with the Holy Spirit as a guarantee that we will make it to that day (Eph. 1:13–14; 2 Cor. 5:5). On that day, Christians will be finally conformed to the image of Christ, in body as well as in spirit. If sin then would be an offense to the character of Christ, so sin now is an offense to the Spirit who promises to bring us to that day.

> Let all bitterness, and wrath, and anger, and clamour,
> and evil speaking, be put away from you, with all mal-
> ice (Eph. 4:31)

Paul provides no cushion for sin. The believer is to reject all such ungodly attitudes. Bitterness is the attitude which remembers the sins (real or imagined) of another. As my father taught, bitterness has good study habits—review, review, review. But love does not keep a record of wrongs. Rage, or violent outbursts of anger, is prohibited. In a similar way, anger is forbidden. The apostle is here referring to self-centered anger, not the righteous anger just required and commanded in verse 26. Neither is the Christian to participate in brawls, whether verbal or physical. Slander occurs when someone lies about another in an attempt to hurt them. The Christian must reject such behavior, along with every form of malice.

> And be ye kind one to another, tenderhearted, forgiving
> one another, even as God for Christ's sake hath forgiven
> you. (Eph. 4:32)

This was probably one of the first verses I ever memorized. I memorized it as a result of my mother quoting it to me when I squabbled with my brother and sister ("be ye kind one to another, tenderhearted . . ." I was a diligent student of the King James early on).

Our standard for extending forgiveness should be identical to our standard for receiving forgiveness. Just as God forgave us in Christ, so we should forgive each other. Only then will we be obedient to the word of Christ. "But if you do not forgive men their sins, your Father will not forgive your sins" (Matt. 6:15).

This forgiveness cannot be grudging. If it is, it is not true forgiveness. It must be extended with kindness and compassion.

EPHESIANS 5

SUBMISSION AND SACRIFICE

In these politically correct days, whenever we come across passages like this one, expositors rush to instruct the faithful on what it does not mean. But we can spend a lot of time learning what things don't mean. What *does* it mean? How should we live? Let us at least begin there. If we address that correctly, it should head off the most common misconceptions at least.

> Be ye therefore followers of God, as dear children; And walk in love, as Christ also hath loved us, and hath given himself for us an offering and a sacrifice to God for a sweetsmelling savour . . . . (Eph. 5:1–33)

Imitate God, as beloved children would (v. 1)—for that is what you are. Walk in love, the same way Christ loved us

and gave Himself for us sacrificially (v. 2). Sexual unclean-
ness and greed have no place with us (v. 3). The same is true
of low jesting and scurrilous talk, but rather thanksgiving
(v. 4). For be sure of it, the sexually corrupt and the greedy
have no inheritance with Christ (v. 5). Don't be deceived on
this point (v. 6), and we might add that many have been.
Do not partake with or stand next to children of disobedience—God's wrath is coming on them (v. 7). You used to be
darkness, but now you are light. Walk like it (v. 8). The fruit
of the Spirit (which is light) is goodness, righteousness, and
truth (v. 9). Live out and prove what God likes (v. 10). Do
not fellowship with unfruitful darkness, but rather reprove
it (v. 11). You can reprove without itemizing all their deeds,
which are shameful even to recount (v. 12). Light is as light
does; light makes *manifest* (v. 13). This is why God tells the
sleeper to awake (v. 14; cf. Isa. 60:1). Walk intelligently, as
though it were daylight (v. 15). Use your time well because
the days are evil (v. 16). Understand God's will (v. 17).
Don't get drunk on wine, but rather be filled with the Spirit
(v. 18). The description of that Spirit-filling follows—speaking to one another with psalms, hymns, and odes, from the
heart (v. 19). Give thanks for everything to God the Father
in the name of Jesus (v. 20). Submit to one another in the
fear of God (v. 21).

Wives are to take particular care to be submissive to their
own husbands (v. 22). This is because the husband is the
head of the wife, as Christ is the head of the Church (v. 23).
This means that as the Church is subject to Christ, so wives
should be subject to their own husbands in everything (v.
24). Paul then tells husbands to sacrifice themselves for

their wives in love (v. 25). He tells them Christ sacrificed Himself with a cleansing and sanctifying end in view (v. 26). He did this so that His Church would be ultimately purified (v. 27). In this same way, men ought to love their wives (v. 28). Nobody hates his own body, but rather takes care of it (v. 29). We are joined together with Christ, members of His body (v. 30). Paul then cites Genesis—a man will leave his father and mother, be joined to his wife as one flesh with her (v. 31). This is a great mystery, Paul says, but it refers upward to Christ and the Church (v. 32). In the meantime, you men make a point of loving your wives, and you wives make a point of reverencing your husbands (v. 33).

Paul continues to contrast for us the characteristics of the regenerate and the unregenerate. It is a stark contrast, and so he urges us not to be deceived with vain words—the wrath of God is falling upon the children of disobedience, and so we should walk as children of light. The children of light should not be partakers together with the children of disobedience (v. 7). The one group is darkness and the other light (v. 8). The one group is fruitless (v. 11) and the other is fruitful (v. 9). The one is foolish and the other wise (v. 15). The difference between the converted and the unconverted is not to be hunted for in a gray twilight. Wake *up*!

A godless life is like a belly full of wine. The lifestyle of unbelief is lazy, muddy, blurred, indistinct, and full of off-key singing. The lifestyle of the faithful is focused, good, clear, disciplined, and full of light. Paul sees certain things as going together, and he is an apostle, a wise man. Tell me, when you have had too many beers, or too many glasses of wine, do the jokes gradually get cleaner and cleaner? The contrast that the apostle expects us to maintain is a contrast that is impossible to maintain apart from the filling of the Spirit. And we will be filled with *something*.

When we are filled with the Spirit, we see things clearly. When we are filled with the Spirit, everything comes into focus. When we are filled with the Spirit, we are filled with holy *music* (v. 19), we are filled with *thanksgiving* for absolutely everything (v. 20), and we are filled with an attitude of mutual *submission* (v. 21). These three things will also carry over into our marriages.

Submission and sacrifice are the characteristics of Spirit-filled marriage. Apart from the work of the Spirit, this standard for marriage is absolutely impossible. When the Spirit is active, it is impossible not to live this way.

Wives, in the Spirit (full of music, thanksgiving, and deference), obey your husband. Honor and respect him. It is striking that when the apostle sets to work in giving direction for all forms of social relations, he starts with the wives. This is not because wives are the worst; I would argue that it is because the wives are the most important. In all social relations, if this stone doesn't get set properly, nothing else will be straight.

Husbands, in the Spirit (full of music, thanksgiving, and deference), sacrifice yourself for your wife. Give yourself away. Take your models from above you (Christ) and from below you (your own body). This is not to be understood as being willing to sacrifice yourselves some hypothetical day in the far distant future, but rather as laying down your life now.

This is a great mystery, Paul says, but it all resolves in Christ and the Church. As Eve was taken from the side of Adam, so the Church was born when the spear was rammed into the side of Christ. Adam refused to fight the dragon, and Christ did not refuse to do it. Men, as dearly loved children, be imitators of God.

VERSE BY VERSE

In this chapter, Paul is taking his earlier grand themes of cosmic reconciliation and spreading it into all the corners. The most obvious example is that here is his teaching on the nature of the relationship between husband and wife. If God can bring the enmity of Jew and Gentile to a close, then He can certainly do the same with the war between the sexes.

> Be ye therefore followers of God, as dear children (Eph. 5:1)

It is in the nature of children to imitate their parents. This is even more the case when the parents love their children dearly and display that love. In the same way, we are to imitate our Father in the heavens. He loves us with a perfect love. He has made us His children (1 John 3:1). Our imitation of Him should be as natural as that of a beloved child to a loving parent.

> And walk in love, as Christ also hath loved us, and hath given himself for us an offering and a sacrifice to God for a sweetsmelling savour. (Eph. 5:2)

Because God loves us, any imitation of Him will result in a life of love. This love will not be sporadic. Rather, it will be a constant characteristic of our lives.

As we imitate God, we are not asked to imitate theological abstractions. We have a concrete example of God's love for us in Christ's death on the cross. This death was a fragrant offering and sacrifice to God. It is also an example of love for us to imitate. To imitate Christ's love on the cross is not to deny the unique sacrificial significance of His death. As Christians, we are to imitate how Christ lived and how He died. We cannot duplicate the sacrifice of Christ, but we are still commanded to imitate it.

> But fornication, and all uncleanness, or covetousness,
> let it not be once named among you, as becometh saints
> (Eph. 5:3)

There are certain things mentioned here that are inconsistent with the imitation of God. These are greed, impurity, and sexual immorality. Greed is lust for material possession. We live in quite a materialistic society and it is regrettable that the biblical prohibition of greed is so rarely applied within the Church. The word in Greek for impurity here indicates profligate, luxurious living. And sexual immorality refers to any sexual activity apart from or in violation of the covenant of marriage. Among God's holy people there must not even be a hint of such things.

> Neither filthiness, nor foolish talking, nor jesting, which
> are not convenient: but rather giving of thanks. (Eph. 5:4)

Equally inconsistent with an imitation of God are certain verbal improprieties. Christians are not to be gross, silly, or vulgar. Think of junior high bathroom humor. Christians are not to be crass in their talk. These characteristics are out of place. But it is not enough to remove the evil. It must always be replaced with something else. In this case, thanksgiving is to replace the vulgarity.

> For this ye know, that no whoremonger, nor unclean person, nor covetous man, who is an idolater, hath any inheritance in the kingdom of Christ and of God. (Eph. 5:5)

There will be no sin in the coming kingdom. Those who think to keep their sin and still inherit the kingdom totally misunderstand the nature of grace. Grace is not given to keep us in sin, albeit forgiven. It is given to *liberate* us from it. If immorality, impurity, or greed are characteristic of a man's life, then that man is not a Christian. He has no part in the inheritance of the kingdom of Christ. Paul comments here that greed is the same thing as idolatry. A greedy man considers material things to be more important than God. He places the created ahead of the Creator—which is the essence of idolatry.

> Let no man deceive you with vain words: for because of these things cometh the wrath of God upon the children of disobedience. Be not ye therefore partakers with them. (Eph. 5:6–7)

Those who live in sin naturally are excluded from the kingdom. Paul warns of the tendency to water down the standards of holiness associated with the kingdom. Such attempts are deceptive. The words used to deceive are empty. Even if words like *grace* are used to excuse ongoing rebellion, Paul's point is clear.

God is angry with such behavior, and the day is coming when that anger will be poured out. Those who are disobedient will be judged. Paul instructs the Ephesians to refuse partnership with those who are headed for that destruction. Christians are to love the lost and are to be a witness to them. Love them, speak to them, and reach out to them. Do everything except *join* them.

> For ye were sometimes darkness, but now are ye light in the Lord: walk as children of light (Eph. 5:8)

There is no way that light can be allied with darkness. Because Christians were once darkness, but are now light, that distinction must be visibly maintained.

Paul here instructs them to live out what they are. Because the Ephesians are children of light, they should live as children of light. The same applies to us.

> (For the fruit of the Spirit is in all goodness and righteousness and truth) (Eph. 5:9)

Living as children of light involves exhibiting the fruit of the Spirit. In order to be accurately described as fruit, the resultant characteristics must be natural and organic. They must proceed from a heart that is similar in kind.

The fruit mentioned here consists of goodness, righteousness, and truth. One of them (goodness) shows up in Paul's more famous list in Galatians 5:22. The other two are equally consistent with that list.

> Proving what is acceptable unto the Lord. (Eph. 5:10)

Paul teaches that we are to find out what pleases the Lord, clearly implying that the Lord *can* be pleased with us. A Christian who has compromised with sin cannot experience that pleasure. A Christian who has made a formal theological alliance with sin ("nobody's perfect") is in the same position.

It is not enough to be aware that God can be pleased. We are taught to find out what pleases the Lord. The clear implication is that we are to do what pleases Him. We are to follow the example of the Thessalonians. "Finally, brothers, we instructed you how to live *in order to please God, as in fact you are living*. Now we ask you and urge you in the Lord Jesus to do this more and more" (1 Thess. 4:1).

> And have no fellowship with the unfruitful works of darkness, but rather reprove them. (Eph. 5:11)

Again, there is a clear call for Christians to be separate from the world. There is to be no connection between the fruitful lives of Christians and the utter fruitlessness of evil. Because all types of fruitfulness are a blessing from God, there is no way to rebel against God without ultimately rebelling against fruitfulness. Deeds of darkness are always fruitless. Christians, by the example of their fruitful lives, expose evil actions for what they are.

> For it is a shame even to speak of those things which are done of them in secret. (Eph. 5:12)

Apparently it is possible to expose wickedness without going into graphic detail. If wickedness is exposed through godly example, nothing more is needed. But if Christians try to expose wickedness by detailing what the disobedient do in secret, the exposure can backfire. The exposure becomes something the ungodly can mock, and they do. The infidel can ridicule the believer's obvious inexperience with the things he is talking about. If he is experienced, he can be charged with hypocrisy ("how do *you* know about these things?"), and if inexperienced, he can be mocked as a naif.

> But all things that are reproved are made manifest by the light: for whatsoever doth make manifest is light. Wherefore he saith, Awake thou that sleepest, and arise from the dead, and Christ shall give thee light. (Eph. 5:13–14)

The exposure of wickedness is accomplished by the simple presence of light. Light makes everything visible; nothing more is necessary.

The light is Christ, and He shines through the children of light. As the light strikes non-Christians, their sin is exposed. He calls on the sleeper to rise from the dead. If they respond, Christ will shine on them. Paul is using the text in a particular way, and he also claims that it was the intention of God that it be used this way—*wherefore he saith.*

> See then that ye walk circumspectly, not as fools, but as wise (Eph. 5:15)

Christians are to avoid partnership with darkness, yet they are to have an effect on it. It is a task that calls for balance and wisdom. In order to live wisely in this way, it is necessary to pay close attention to how you live.

> Redeeming the time, because the days are evil. (Eph. 5:16)

Because the days are evil, opportunities to shine the light will not be abundant. Consequently, every possible opportunity must be seized.

> Wherefore be ye not unwise, but understanding what the will of the Lord is. (Eph. 5:17)

Here the Lord's will is to be understood as His revealed will. In other words, God has told us how He wants us to live and it is our responsibility to comprehend that revelation.

Paul is not referring to the specific will of God, with reference to particular individuals. He is not commanding us to understand whether we should take this job or that one, or marry this person or the other one.

God does have a specific plan for each individual (e.g. Eph. 2:10), but we are not commanded to discover what it is before we do it. Our lives are a mist and we cannot say what tomorrow will bring. Rather, if we understand and obey God's revealed moral will, He will keep us within the boundaries of His specific will.

> And be not drunk with wine, wherein is excess; but be filled with the Spirit (Eph. 5:18)

Drinking is not condemned here, although drunkenness is. Occasional drunkenness is prohibited because it leads to debauchery. Debauchery is to be understood as a thorough corruption of moral character.

Notice that the prohibition is placed alongside a godly alternative. God doesn't want Christians to be wine-filled, because he wants them to be Spirit-filled, and the two are inconsistent. Just as a mother says *no* to candy for her children right before dinner, so God says *no* to us. The mother says *no* because the candy will ruin the dinner she has prepared, which is far better. In the same way, God denies us certain things which will ruin our appetite for the better things He has prepared.

The better thing here is the *filling of the Spirit*. The common translation, *filled with the Spirit*, makes it appear as though we are empty vessels and the Spirit is a sort of spiritual fluid that fills us up. A better translation is *filled by means of the Spirit*. This is consistent with previous instances of that construction in Ephesians (2:18; 2:22; 3:5) and consistent with what Paul teaches elsewhere. Such a translation indicates that the Spirit is the *agent* doing the filling, not the substance with which we are filled. This raises the question, obviously, of what it is that fills us.

In Colossians 3:16, there is a parallel passage to this one. In it, the Colossians are instructed to "let the word of Christ dwell . . . richly." The effects of that indwelling are "psalms and hymns and spiritual songs," which are also the result of this Spirit-filling here in Ephesians. If we put the two passages together, we get something like this: "Let the word of Christ dwell in you richly by means of the Spirit." The word of Christ is what we are filled with; the indwelling Spirit is the one who does the pouring and filling.

> Speaking to yourselves in psalms and hymns and spiritual songs, singing and making melody in your heart to the Lord (Eph. 5:19)

When Christians are filled by means of the Spirit, certain characteristics are visible in their lives. In the Greek, it is clear that verses 19–22 are a description of the Spirit-filled life.

So we are to address one another with various forms of spiritual music—psalms and hymns and spiritual songs. We do not sing in order to become filled. We are to sing because we have been filled, and we need to overflow. The former makes Christian music a form of mere psychological manipulation. The latter understands it as an expression of heart-filled thanks. We are to sing to one another. This should be the result of hearts that sing to the Lord. This is good for your soul.

> Giving thanks always for all things unto God and the Father in the name of our Lord Jesus Christ (Eph. 5:20)

Again, the direction of prayer is always to the Father. It is accomplished through (in the name of) Jesus Christ. The prayer in this instance is a prayer of thanksgiving. Thanks should be rendered all the time for everything. Christians are to rejoice all the time, in every circumstance, and for every circumstance.

> Submitting yourselves one to another in the fear of God. (Eph. 5:21)

Mutual submission is also an indication of the Spirit's working. This attitude of humility is not expressed because of an excessively high view of one's fellows, but because of a reverence for God. Because God is honored, those in Christ are also honored.

> Wives, submit yourselves unto your own husbands, as unto the Lord. (Eph. 5:22)

Grammatically, this requirement is part of the preceding instruction. The submission of a wife to her husband is part of the greater submission of Christian to Christian—which is evidence of the Spirit's work. Nevertheless the unique authority of husband over wife is clearly taught here. Modern feminism (even if decked out in evangelical terminology) is utterly absent from this passage. Equally absent is the notion that husbands are to be little dictators. The wife is here instructed to be submissive to her husband as she would be to the Lord.

> For the husband is the head of the wife, even as Christ is the head of the church: and he is the saviour of the body. (Eph. 5:23)

What Christ is to the Church, the husband is to his wife, although on a much humbler level. Nevertheless, headship is characteristic of both relationships. When it is said that Christ is the head of the Church, His body, marriage provides us with a good illustration of it. Christ is not the head of the body in the same way that my head is the head of my body. He is the head of the body in the same way that I am the head of my wife.

Thus we see that the "bride of Christ" and the "body of Christ" are not two metaphors describing two separate realities. They are two descriptions of the same reality. We are the body of Christ because we are the bride of Christ. He is the Savior of the body, the Savior of the bride.

> Therefore as the church is subject unto Christ, so let
> the wives be to their own husbands in every thing.
> (Eph. 5:24)

Wives are to submit to their husbands in all things. This is not possible unless the wife's entire demeanor is submissive. Her pattern for submission is the submission of the church to Jesus Christ. This does not require the submission of one woman to all men. It is one woman and one man—a relationship that protects her from the oppression of other men.

> Husbands, love your wives, even as Christ also loved
> the church, and gave himself for it (Eph. 5:25)

In a similar way, husbands have a pattern to guide them in their relationships with their wives. Wives are to be to their husbands what the Church is to Christ. Husbands are to be to their wives what Christ is to the Church. It is true that the husband is given authority, but the authority is limited by the God-given pattern. Husbands have been given authority to love their wives, along with the authority to sacrifice themselves for their wives. Authority in the home that is not loving and self-sacrificial is an unbiblical authority. It is interesting to note that husbands are told to love their wives, while wives are not told to love their husbands. The primary responsibility of wives is submission and respect. The primary responsibility of husbands is love and self-sacrifice.

> That he might sanctify and cleanse it with the washing
> of water by the word (Eph. 5:26)

Christ gave Himself up in order to be able to set the Church apart, i.e., to make her holy. He cleanses her of all defilement. In a similar way, husbands are responsible for the spiritual condition of their wives. The Word of God needs to occupy a central place in the home so that it can have its cleansing effect.

> That he might present it to himself a glorious church,
> not having spot, or wrinkle, or any such thing; but that
> it should be holy and without blemish. (Eph. 5:27)

Christ loved the Church, not because she was lovely but in order to make her lovely. Biblical love is not conditional upon the loveliness of the recipient. It is unconditional and produces loveliness in the recipient. Christ loved the Church in this way so that the same Church could be presented to Himself radiant, without spot or any other kind of blemish. Husbands are to assume a similar responsibility for the spiritual loveliness of their wives.

> So ought men to love their wives as their own bodies.
> He that loveth his wife loveth himself. (Eph. 5:28)

Not only are husbands to love their wives as Christ loved the Church, they are to love their wives as they love themselves. The latter instruction is simply an application of the great commandment ("love your neighbor as yourself") to marriage. As a man naturally cares for himself, he should also care for his wife. If he does so, he will be greatly blessed in return. A man who truly gives himself to his wife will not regret it. He who loves his wife loves himself. A man who loves his wife this way will have difficulty in outgiving her.

> For no man ever yet hated his own flesh; but nour-
> isheth and cherisheth it, even as the Lord the church
> (Eph. 5:29)

Husbands ought to care for their own bodies (their wives) as they care for their own bodies (their own bodies). If a man cares for his wife as he cares for himself, she is secure. This is because no one ever hated his own body. Everyone cares for his own body like Christ cares for the Church. The instruction here is to use that natural tendency to care for yourself as the standard for caring for your wife.

The passage also clearly contradicts the modern psychological nonsense that "before you can love someone else,
you have to love yourself." Paul assumes a natural level
of self-love and requires that the same kind of love be
directed outward.

> For we are members of his body, of his flesh, and of his
> bones. (Eph. 5:30)

Individual Christians are various members in the body of
Christ—which He cares for in a loving, self-sacrificial way.

> For this cause shall a man leave his father and mother,
> and shall be joined unto his wife, and they two shall be
> one flesh. (Eph. 5:31)

The quotation is from Genesis 2:24. When a man leaves
home to marry, he is forming a completely new family.
He leaves the old family and establishes a new one. This
happens when he leaves home and is sexually united to a
woman within the boundaries of the marriage covenant.

> This is a great mystery: but I speak concerning Christ
> and the church. (Eph. 5:32)

Paul has an exalted view of marriage and of sex within
marriage. He is saying here that the unity experienced by
husband and wife in making love is a dim picture of the
unity that the Church has with Christ. Sex is respected by
Christians because of what it represents. Sexual immorality

is opposed because of how it distorts or vandalizes that picture. Both fornication and adultery are *lies* about the character of Christ.

> Nevertheless let every one of you in particular so love
> his wife even as himself; and the wife see that she reverence her husband. (Eph. 5:33)

In summing up his teaching on marriage, Paul reiterates the two basic points. Husbands—love your wives. Wives—respect your husbands.

EPHESIANS 6

THE TREASURIES OF GRACE

Paul concludes this epistle with some pointed ethical instructions for various groups in the church, with a soaring and inspired passage about the right use of the armor of God, some of his usual greetings, as well as with a request for prayer. The request is that he would be as bold as he ought to be—he is asking for prayer that *he* would put on the full armor of God. He is not, after decades of ministry, wrestling with stage fright, or with a bad case of butterflies. He knows what happens to him whenever the gospel is declared with power. When he puts on that armor, battle is near.

Children, obey your parents in the Lord: for this is right. Honour thy father and mother; (which is the first

> commandment with promise;) That it may be well with
> thee, and thou mayest live long on the earth. And, ye
> fathers, provoke not your children to wrath: but bring
> them up in the nurture and admonition of the Lord . . . .
> (Eph. 6:1–24)

Children are told to obey their parents. This is the right thing to do (v. 1). Paul then cites the commandment to honor father and mother, and adds the point that this is the first commandment with a promise attached (v. 2). He picks up the promise and expands it to encompass the whole earth (v. 3). Fathers, for their part, are told not to exasperate their kids, but to provide them with a Christian education and upbringing (v. 4).

Slaves are told to obey their earthly masters with fear and trembling, as rendered to Christ (v. 5). They are told not to work for show, but rather with whole-hearted service to Christ (v. 6). The service they offer is for the Lord, not for men (v. 7). They should know that however any man works, free or slave, is reckoned up by the Lord (v. 8). Masters are to have the same mentality. They should not threaten, and they must remember that they have a Master in heaven, one who is not impressed by earthly status (v. 9).

Paul then tells his brothers to be strong in the Lord, in the power of His might (v. 10). They are told to put on the entire armor of God, in order that they might stand against the devil's wiles (v. 11). Our fight is not primarily an earthly one; we fight against principalities and powers, against the rulers of this world's darkness, and against wickedness in high places (v. 12). This is why it is important to take up the full armor of God and to stand in the evil day (v. 13). Stand therefore with the belt of truth and breastplate of righteousness (v. 14). Your feet should be shod with gospel boots (v. 15). These boots are the gospel of peace and they are part of our *armor*. Take the shield of faith, which extinguishes the fiery darts of the wicked (v. 16). Then take the helmet of salvation, and the sword of the Spirit, which is the Word of God (v. 17), and proceed to the battle, which is the battleground of persevering prayer for all the saints (v. 18). Paul requests prayer for himself in this regard, so that he might unlock the treasuries of the gospel (v. 19). He requests that he might be able to speak boldly, as he ought to (v. 20).

Tychicus is then recommended to them (v. 21), and he will tell the Ephesians how Paul is doing (vv. 21–22). He concludes with a benediction—peace to the brothers and love proceeding from faith, from God the Father and the Lord Jesus (v. 23). Grace to all who love Jesus sincerely (v. 24).

Christian children are to be brought up in an environment or culture that is shaped by the Word of God. They are called to obey their parents in the Lord, which is right. They are told to honor their parents, a commandment from the Old Testament that is given to the Christian children of Ephesus. This passage is one of the best illustrations of how we are to apply the Old Testament authoritatively to our lives now.

Then there is the problem of exasperating fathers. When Paul warns Christian fathers to not be exasperating to their children, he does this because this is one of the faults that Christian fathers are prone to. So *listen* to him. Before you just brush this admonition off and say that of *course* you don't do this, consider that it is possible that this defensive and self-serving attitude is one of the most exasperating things about you. And remember that your children frequently will not be able to explain this to you. First, because they are little and defenseless, and then later because they moved to the East Coast and never call.

What about slaves and masters? God's methods for societal overhaul are reformational, not revolutionary. This is one of the places where we must insist on a policy of not apologizing for the Bible. Christian slaves are told to be obedient. They are told to work hard, offering it to Christ. Whatever their earthly masters do, *He* will honor their labors. Work offered to God is the way to true freedom. This is the biblical way of overthrowing unjust social institutions. Christian masters (assuming then that there were some) are told to internalize the *same* biblical framework. God does not show partiality, and so they should not govern through threats. This being the case, how much more does it apply to employers and employees.

The Ephesians were told earlier to put on the new man. Here they are told to put on the full armor of God, which amounts to the same thing. Every piece of the armor is the Lord Jesus. He is the truth (John 14:6). He is our righteousness (Jer. 23:6). He is the gospel of peace (Isa. 9:6). He is the faithful one in whom we have faith (Rev. 19:11). He is our salvation, which we may wear as a helmet (1 Thess. 5:9). He is the sword of the Spirit (Rev. 19:15), the Word of God (Rev. 19:13; John 1:1–3).

But when you are fitted out in this armor, what do you *do*? First, you should take note of the enemy. You are called to

stand against wiles (v. 11), and since we are fighting wickedness in high places, you should assume the lies are coming down on you from above. Paul then says, three times,
that you should be outfitted so that you may with*stand*
in the evil day (v. 13) and having done all to *stand*. *Stand
therefore* (v. 14). How do you do that? Fitted out, what do
you *do*? You pray for all the saints, and particularly for the
proclamation of the gospel (v. 19).

Paul has already spoken of the mystery of the gospel. It
is as though, Jerome observes, that Paul now says that God
has declared "let the treasuries be opened." He is standing
by the doors of these treasuries (filled beyond our imagina-
tion) and is set to fling them open. But there is a fierce battle by those doors. If they get opened all the way, then the
wickedness in the high places is completely undone.

VERSE BY VERSE
In this chapter, Paul continues to bring the applications
down into the matters of everyday life, and he here applies
these realities to the duties of Christian children, as well as
to the very common institution of domestic slavery. How
does the transformation of the cosmos apply to something
like that? And then he returns to loftier heights and, using
imagery from the prophet Isaiah (Isa. 59:17), discusses our
role in the spiritual war being waged against the principalities and powers.

> Children, obey your parents in the Lord: for this is right.
> (Eph. 6:1)

It is good and proper for children to be obedient to their parents. While a child is in the home, he honors his parents by obeying them. When he leaves home (and starts a new family) the obligation to honor them still remains, although it is now expressed differently (Mark 7:10–13), which is to say, through financial support. Before a child reaches maturity, obedience to parents is a God-given protection and blessing.

> Honour thy father and mother; (which is the first commandment with promise) (Eph. 6:2)

The citation is from Deuteronomy 5:16, the fifth of the Ten Commandments. Paul makes it clear that submission to this commandment by children requires obedience to parents. He also comments that the command comes with a promise. The first four commands do not have any blessings attached to them.

> That it may be well with thee, and thou mayest live long on the earth. (Eph. 6:3)

The promise concerns prosperity and longevity in this life. Because the family is the basic building block of society, the family must be respected if society is to thrive. If the family is to be respected, then parents must be honored by their children.

It is interesting to note that Paul is applying one of the Ten Commandments along with its associated promise to a *Gentile* church. While it must be obeyed, Paul is very clear that the moral law is not the means of salvation. He is equally clear that the tenets of the moral law express the mind of God and should be fully lived out by those who have been forgiven.

> And, ye fathers, provoke not your children to wrath: but bring them up in the nurture and admonition of the Lord. (Eph. 6:4)

Fathers are not to make obedience difficult for their children. They are not to provoke, annoy, or exasperate them. Fathers can violate this instruction by being overly harsh or by teasing too much. Instead of this, fathers are to assume responsibility for the spiritual well-being of their children. Contrary to popular misconceptions, it is not the mother who has this responsibility, even though she may have a greater desire to see that it is done. This responsibility is taken on in the training and instruction of children. The teaching should occur both as situations arise and in a more formal setting. There should be ongoing instruction and a regular devotional teaching time. The father is responsible to see to it that both occur.

> Servants, be obedient to them that are your masters according to the flesh, with fear and trembling, in singleness of your heart, as unto Christ (Eph. 6:5)

Slavery was exceedingly common in the Roman Empire at this time. As Christianity grew, slaves were converted and received into the body of Christ as full members. In Christ, there was to be no difference between slave and free. In the world, however, the distinction remained and it was a difficult problem for the Church. How does the unity of all believers translate into a world where there are masters and slaves, including Christian masters and Christian slaves? All in the same Church?

The answer of the New Testament is plain. Immediate abolitionism, abolition at any cost, was not their answer. What Paul is doing here (and in numerous other passages) is establishing certain principles within the church that would be, in the long run, deeply subversive of slavery as an accepted institution. For those who want to pursue this subject further, they can refer to my *Black and Tan* (pp. 37–39), and to my commentary on Philemon in this series. The bottom line is that, according to Paul, neither slaveholding nor being a slave was sinful in itself. Slavery was, however, a condition where sin could spring up easily—whether it was disobedience on the part of slaves or harshness on the part of masters.

Paul begins by addressing the Christian slaves. They were to work for their earthly masters as for Jesus Christ. This obedience should proceed from the heart. Respect and fear were rendered because of the slave's relationship to Jesus Christ. This attitude should not be adjusted even if the master was also a Christian. Nevertheless, slavery was not a condition Paul thought they should remain in if they had any alternative (1 Cor. 7:21–23).

> Not with eyeservice, as menpleasers; but as the servants of Christ, doing the will of God from the heart (Eph. 6:6)

Christian slaves are obedient because they are working for Christ, so it should make no difference whether their earthly master is present or not. To work in this way is to do the will of God from the heart. Consequently, the slave is to work obediently, whether he is supervised or not.

> With good will doing service, as to the Lord, and not
> to men: Knowing that whatsoever good thing any man
> doeth, the same shall he receive of the Lord, whether he
> be bond or free. (Eph. 6:7–8)

The Christian slave is to conduct himself as a slave of Christ and not as a slave of men. A slave who works in this way is exhibiting true liberation and true freedom. In working for the Lord, the slave has confidence that he is not working for a harsh master, regardless of how ungodly his *earthly* master may be. The Lord shows no partiality, and He rewards slaves and free equally, provided they have done what is good.

The Christian slave is therefore not trapped by his circumstances, and he demonstrates it through his obedience.

> And, ye masters, do the same things unto them, for-
> bearing threatening: knowing that your Master also is
> in heaven; neither is there respect of persons with him.
> (Eph. 6:9)

Paul also wants the attitudes of Christian masters to be godly. Notice he does not command Christian masters to free their slaves immediately. He *does* command them to cultivate a certain attitude. First, they are to treat their slaves "in the same way," i.e., with the same desire to work for God that the Christian slaves were instructed to have. Secondly, they are not to rule through threats and intimidation. The reason they may not threaten is that they also have a Master who lives in the heavens. This Master does not show partiality and could easily take the side of a slave if the master were being harsh with him. Both master and slave were required to remember that in Christ there is neither slave nor free. For the slave, this realization translated into hard-working obedience, and for the master it translated into humble, kind oversight.

> Finally, my brethren, be strong in the Lord, and in the power of his might. (Eph. 6:10)

What follows is a discussion of spiritual warfare. Paul prefaces the discussion by reminding the Ephesians of the only place where it is possible for them to wage such a war, and of the only source of the strength available for them. That position is *in the Lord*. The power for fighting comes from Him alone. In the verses that follow, the more we learn about the nature of the conflict, the more it becomes necessary to remember this first instruction.

> Put on the whole armour of God, that ye may be able to stand against the wiles of the devil. (Eph. 6:11)

Part of the conflict is defensive. The devil's machinations must be resisted. In order to resist them effectively, the

Christian must have on only the full armor of God. Having only half the armor is as useless as having none at all. Everything Paul mentions here is necessary in order to make an effective stand.

> For we wrestle not against flesh and blood, but against principalities, against powers, against the rulers of the darkness of this world, against spiritual wickedness in high places. (Eph. 6:12)

Spiritual warfare is not conducted against physical enemies. This means that non-Christians are not the enemy in the conflict—they are flesh and blood. They are rather what the fight is *over*. A Christian who sees non-Christians as the enemy, rather than as prisoners and slaves of the enemy, has a mistaken understanding of the conflict. By the same token, spiritual warfare is not conducted against our own desires. We, too, are flesh and blood. Spiritual warfare is waged against spiritual enemies.

Many Christians make the mistake of seeing the spiritual conflict solely in terms of God and Satan—with Satan being considered as God's opposite. This notion is mistaken on two counts. First, God has no opposite. He is the uncreated Creator, and Satan is not on the same level at all. Secondly, Christians tend to lump all forces of evil under one heading and call it "Satan." Paul teaches us the opposite. In this section, he mentions five types of opponents. He mentions the devil, rulers, authorities, world rulers, and spiritual armies of evil. We know very little about the enemy, and so we have to be strong in the Lord and to make sure we have all our armor on.

> Wherefore take unto you the whole armour of God,
> that ye may be able to withstand in the evil day, and
> having done all, to stand. (Eph. 6:13)

Paul wants Christians to stand firm in the initial onslaught and, after they have fought all they can, to still be standing. Again, Paul warns us that in order to be able to do this, a believer must be equipped with all God's armor. With such equipment, the prepared Christian does not need to fear the day of evil. He is ready to stand.

> Stand therefore, having your loins girt about with
> truth, and having on the breastplate of righteousness
> (Eph. 6:14)

The belt held the sword and kept clothes from impeding the movements of the warrior. The Christian's belt is truth. There is some question over whether this refers to doctrinal truth or truthfulness of character. While it is true the two cannot do without each other, I am inclined to think it refers to truthfulness of character. A commitment to truth enables the Christian to fight effectively.

The breastplate protects all the vital organs. In the same way, the righteous character of the warrior/saint protects him from the assaults of the enemy.

> And your feet shod with the preparation of the gospel of
> peace (Eph. 6:15)

This piece of equipment (gospel boots) is for offensive use against the enemy. The gospel produces readiness to share the gospel. That readiness should be fitted on our feet. As we preach the gospel to those ensnared by the enemy, we strike a blow against the enemy.

> Above all, taking the shield of faith, wherewith ye shall be able to quench all the fiery darts of the wicked (Eph. 6:16).

We can deduce the nature of the "fiery darts" from what it takes to extinguish them. If faith puts out the darts, then the darts are probably best considered doubts that come from the evil one.

So when doubts start coming at you, the only appropriate response is to reject them in faith. Questions should be answered, with doubts rejected and ignored. Doubts, by their very nature, cannot be answered, but only rejected. The equipment for doing this is the shield of faith.

> And take the helmet of salvation, and the sword of the Spirit, which is the word of God (Eph. 6:17)

There is no protection from the enemy if one belongs to the enemy. In order to be freed from his bondage, an individual must be saved by God from the power and bondage of sin. If he is, he may put on the helmet along with the rest of the armor.

The Scriptures are to be our weapon. In spiritual conflict, we should wield it as our Lord did, placing ourselves in submission to it (Matt. 4:1–11). Jesus did not quote Scripture at Satan. He quoted Scripture, applying it to Himself in the face of Satan's attack. Because the Word of God is our weapon, it is essential to trust it fully. A high view of

Scripture, which holds to its absolute authority, is necessary for success in spiritual warfare.

> Praying always with all prayer and supplication in the Spirit, and watching thereunto with all perseverance and supplication for all saints (Eph. 6:18)

Prayer is the battleground. The battleground is not evangelism, and not preaching and teaching. Those are the places where we reap the fruits of victory. They are not the places where we win the victory. Victory is won in prayer under the control of the Spirit of God.

All types of prayers and requests are included. What prompts the prayer does not matter. If it is controlled by the Spirit, it will be used by Him in the conflict.

Prayer should not be dull and confused. The praying Christian should keep in mind what he is doing and stay alert. Again, prayer is on behalf of the saints. The best way to benefit non-Christians through prayer is to pray for Christians.

> And for me, that utterance may be given unto me, that I may open my mouth boldly, to make known the mystery of the gospel (Eph. 6:19)

Paul by this time had been an apostle of Christ for decades. Nevertheless, he still wanted Christians to support him in prayer in two areas. First, he wanted Christians to pray for the words to be used whenever he opened his mouth to proclaim Christ. Paul did not depend on a canned or memorized message.

The second thing he wanted prayer for was boldness. When he declared the mystery of the gospel, he needed to be given fearlessness. This was not because he had stage fright, or got butterflies at the thought of speaking to large groups. It was because the mystery concerned the union of Jew and Gentile in Christ. It was this part of Paul's message that regularly got him into serious trouble (see Acts 22:21–22). Consequently, it was just here that he needed fearlessness.

> For which I am an ambassador in bonds: that therein I
> may speak boldly, as I ought to speak. (Eph. 6:20)

It was because of this mystery that Paul was imprisoned at the time of writing. Proclaiming truth in a world that loves falsehood will always have negative consequences. Paul repeats his request that the Ephesians pray for fearlessness in him as he declares the message.

> But that ye also may know my affairs, and how I do,
> Tychicus, a beloved brother and faithful minister in the
> Lord, shall make known to you all things (Eph. 6:21)

Tychicus was close to Paul and labored faithfully together with him. He was apparently the one who would carry this letter to the Ephesians and would then supply them with the personal news about Paul that was not contained in the letter.

> Whom I have sent unto you for the same purpose, that
> ye might know our affairs, and that he might comfort
> your hearts. (Eph. 6:22)

Paul sent Tychicus for two reasons. One was to give the news about Paul and his associates. The other was so that Tychicus could be a personal encouragement to them.

> Peace be to the brethren, and love with faith, from God
> the Father and the Lord Jesus Christ. (Eph. 6:23)

Paul concludes with a blessing that originates with the Father and the Son. The blessing calls for peace, love, and faith.

> Grace be with all them that love our Lord Jesus Christ in
> sincerity. Amen. (Eph. 6:24)

Those who persevere in their love for Jesus Christ can count on the grace of God. Their love does not earn the grace—otherwise grace would not be grace. Rather, grace enables us to love and in turn God gives more grace. This blessing of grace is available to anyone who will love the Lord.

www.ingramcontent.com/pod-product-compliance
Lightning Source LLC
Chambersburg PA
CBHW022005090426
42741CB00007B/906